D1034004

DIARY OF A COMPANY MAN

DIARY OF A COMPANY MAN
Losing a Job, Finding a Life

JAMES S. KUNEN

Lyons Press
Guilford, Connecticut
An imprint of Globe Pequot Press

Lyons Press is an imprint of Globe Pequot Press.

Text design: Sheryl Kober
Layout artist: Kirsten Livingston
Project editor: Kristen Mellitt

Library of Congress Cataloging-in-Publication Data is available on file.

ISBN 978-0-7627-7045-8

Printed in the United States of America

10 9 8 7 6 5 4 3 2 1

To the dream girl who is, incredibly, my wife, Lisa;
Halley, our daughter;
and Johnny, our son;

and

to the memory of my grandparents,
Isadore Kunen, Sophie Chafetz
Helen Goldberger and Jacob Litter,
brave young men and women
who dared to leave their homes and families
to go to America.

CONTENTS

I. That Was Then

Consider the lilies, how they grow: they toil not, neither do they spin; yet I say unto you, Even Solomon in all his glory was not arrayed like one of these.

—Luke 12:27

Where should I begin?

In 1968, when I was nineteen, I wrote a book about being nineteen and trying to change the world—or at least find a new way to live in it. It was called *The Strawberry Statement*, and it gave voice to what a lot of people my age were hoping: that our generation would be different. We wouldn't care so much about careers, status, and material things. We'd be less greedy, more kind, less alienated, more true to ourselves. The book was well received. Critics, most of them over thirty and accustomed to being the object of the baby boomers' scorn, especially liked the author's Generation Gap–spanning perspective. "To say that youth is what's happening is absurd," I wrote on page one. "It's always been happening. Everyone is nineteen, only at different times."

This is a different time. When this book is published, I will be sixty-three, *inshallah* (God willing), as the Arab immigrants I tutor like to say. Sixty-three! How did this happen?

Let me put it this way: Once, my son and I were standing in a cemetery as a man's gravestone was about to be unveiled—about to be. But first a rabbi was talking, at length—about the man, and his life, and life itself, and God, and the Jewish people, and the Torah, or maybe the Talmud, and what wise men had said about these things in the past, in Hebrew and in English. It was a very hot day. As the rabbi talked, I turned to my then-teenage son and whispered, "How can life be so short when this speech is so long?"

Time doesn't fly. It just never stops. And the next thing you know, it's now.

Now I find myself at this place called Too Young to Retire and Too Old to Hire, and there's a huge crowd here, a regular Woodstock, with more arriving all the time. Many of us grudgingly made a deal to sell our time on Earth to the Corporation, only to be informed abruptly that the Corporation would no longer be buying. How did *that* happen?

Step by step.

Three years out of college, I wrote an article for *The New York Times Magazine*[1] about how my privileged upper-middle-class friends and I were coming to grips with the fact that we would not be young forever, and that to make a life we would have to make a living—something we'd been avoiding. Embarking on a career seemed to spell an end to our youth and our freedom, I explained. By not working toward a career we were also steering clear of the System, within which success and exploitation, work and war, were all of a piece in our minds. ("Work! Study! Get ahead! Kill!" we used to chant at antiwar demonstrations.) And anyway, we were terrified of working as hard as our fathers, charter subscribers to the Protestant Ethic: Pay now, fly later. But, I wrote at the age of twenty-four,

> *The pressure mounts to make your deal, some sort of compromise between the quest for authentic experience and the need for identity, between adventure and security . . . And as we find idealistic gratification hard to come by, materialistic gratification becomes more attractive. I used to think I could stop the Vietnam War; then I thought I'd get realistic: By working with delinquents, I'd save them from lives of crime. Finding that beyond my power, I resolved to show them a good time. My success in pursuit of even that modest goal was equivocal. After several months as a supervisor and associate of juvenile delinquents it came to me that I'd feel somehow more confident if I had a big car. . . . As my Columbia classmate Dave Warren says, "Whatever else you say about those bourgeois comforts, they sure are comfortable." And they can be habit-forming. After the hook, the line and sinker are easy. . . .*

---

1 "The Rebels of '70: Confessions of a Middle-Class Drifter," *New York Times*, October 28, 1973.

Now more and more holdouts are becoming late-signers. The question is: Will we become indistinguishable from our parents?

I was just talking to a friend of mine, who said, "I'm much happier now that I'm not 'a radical.' I stopped feeling guilty over just being alive in America."

And I said, "My father always held to the belief that young people would eventually abandon their idealistic visions and come around to appreciating the verities—like the overwhelming importance of money."

"Your father sounds like a very wise man," she said.

II. Diary of a Company Man

In the sweat of thy face shalt thou eat bread, till thou return unto the ground; for out of it wast thou taken: for dust thou art, and unto dust shalt thou return.

—Genesis 3:19

Monday, October 7, 2002

Working on my column, "Diary of a Company Man," for the AOL Time Warner employee magazine, I try to ignore the roaring and screeching of the ventilation equipment on the rooftop five stories below my window. It sounds like the engines of a jet about to begin its charge down the runway for takeoff. I can practically smell the jet fuel, feel the vibrations, see the flaps going up and down for a final check. I can feel the great winged machine straining at its locked wheels, its massive metal body shuddering in anticipation of soaring free, but the takeoff never comes.

I get up to look out the window and notice that the seat of my black Naugahyde desk chair bears my imprint: two kidney-shaped depressions separated by a crease. If I were to be struck by a bus tonight, this fossilized remnant of me would survive. *He made an impression here. He made a difference.*

"Diary of a Company Man" is an ironic title for my column, a little joke I share with my readers to show we are on the same side. I'm obviously not a "company man." No one is. The term fell out of use decades ago. It referred to someone who defined himself as a member of a particular company, who valued himself as the company was valued, who was loyal to the company and trusted the company to be loyal to him. Hard to imagine.

No doubt in some of the more productive precincts of AOL Time Warner there are people who take great pride in the particular boat where they pull an oar—at HBO, at CNN, Warner Bros., maybe Time Inc.—but in Corporate Communications, not so much. Of course, you can't go by me. I've been cast against type, and, never having aspired to be where I am, try to think of my work as strictly my day job, even though I have no night job. But the attitude—*This is all bullshit; I just do it for the money*—is so much the norm here that I sometimes think how nice it would be to work shoulder to shoulder with true-believing teammates. I could turn to a colleague, look her in the eye, and say, "We're going to build the best darned international media and entertainment conglomerate the world has ever seen!" And not laugh.

The funny thing is, no one has to tell me what to write. I know my job is to encourage employees (or "-ees," in HR shorthand) to believe that they are valued members of a cool and respected company. I give some recognition to the rank and file—"worker bees," as they're referred to by HR people—any three hundred of whom might get paid as much all together as our CEO. I celebrate their effort, their intelligence, and their integrity—help them to feel that they are appreciated, not viewed as nonentities to be exploited and then tossed away.

Still, I prefer not to think of myself as a propagandist. Writing for the company magazine is no different from writing a column for a newspaper in a medium-size city—AOL Time Warner has ninety thousand employees worldwide—except that I can write only about good news. Rather than bridle at this constraint, I see it as a challenge. It requires keen observation to find good news, and the effort requires the cultivation of a positive outlook that can be quite bracing for someone inclined by nature to a darker view.

For example, I recently went to a NASCAR race, the MBNA All-American Heroes 400 at the Dover International Speedway in Delaware, in order to write a column about our subsidiary Turner Broadcasting's cutting-edge techniques for televising auto races.

This is what I saw:

It was Armed Forces Appreciation Day; 140,000 white people—not one of them Jewish, I swear—filled a grandstand hundreds of yards long, and every single one was clutching a little American flag. (They left the Confederate flags outside on their pickups and RVs.) Before the race began, some Army troops rode slowly around the track, standing at attention in the back of personnel carriers, saluting, the tips of their white-gloved fingers touching smartly angled black berets. The enormous crowd thunderously chanted *U-S-A! U-S-A!*, rhythmically waving their flags in unison as they shouted each kick-ass letter. The Spirit of the Nation electrified the air. Leni Riefenstahl would have felt right at home.

You fucking idiots are going to follow George Bush right over a cliff, and then you're going to say you were misled, and sold out, and stabbed in the back, I was thinking. *Well, don't come complaining to me, because if you opened your eyes you could see that he's lying to you.*

This was the day I realized that people *like* wars. If they didn't, why would we have them all the time? War is not a last resort. It's not a dreaded necessity. It's something people jump right into, given the opportunity. As we say in business, there is a very low barrier to entry.

That's what I saw. And this is what I wrote in "Diary of a Company Man":[2]

> One thing I really like about people—and I don't like every-thing about them, believe me—but one thing I do like is they always find a way to play. Show human beings a cliff and a river, and the next thing you know somebody's doing full gain-ers—just for fun; there's no other reason to do them. Or take cars: No sooner were they invented, practically, than drivers were stomping pedal to the metal, seeing how fast they could go. In 1904, Henry Ford himself set a world speed record of 91.37 mph. Excuse my dust!
>
> Jump ahead a century and you find NASCAR, with the help of Turner Broadcasting System's TNT network, growing faster than any other American sports organization in atten-dance and TV ratings. . . .
>
> To some, auto racing may seem pointless—but that's no reason not to like it. After all, what distinguishes us from the

---

2 "TNT: Vroom! Vroom!" *AOL Time Warner Keywords Magazine*, November 2002.

lower animals if not opposable thumbs and pointless activities? Gentlemen, start your engines!

How did a youthful idealist end up as a corporate flack? God, I don't know. It's not something I planned.

To find an explanation, we'll need to delve further back in my diary.

Thursday, March 16, 2000

Through a series of exigencies and contingencies, and the occasional exercise of what for the sake of convenience let's call free will, I find myself attending a meeting of middle managers from across Time Warner's media and entertainment empire. The earnest young men and women around me are discussing one of the company's core values—innovation. They cite as a sterling example the fact that *Teen People* has come up with a way to get 4,500 kids to serve as unpaid "Trend Spotters," who send in a constant stream of information the magazine uses to help advertisers identify and exploit teenagers' desires. I feel like I'm on a bad acid trip.

"Get out! Get out while you can!" my friend Larry Lane, an itinerant English grad student, would tell me, if he hadn't died at thirty-two.

"This is great! Stay there and learn how the world works," my friend John Short, a great lawyer, would advise me, if he hadn't died at thirty-five.

My father would have been so pleased that I'm here, I'm thinking. Should that matter?

I'm on my own.

Until now, I've spent my working life as a child-care worker, then a journalist, then a defense attorney for the indigent, then a journalist again, always searching for a way to do good, do well, and feel like

I'm not acting—or at least feel like I'm playing myself. A few weeks ago I was still at *People* magazine, assigning and editing articles about politics, crime, sports—anything except celebrities. I was the *People* editor in charge of everything that was no longer important to *People*.

When I started out as a writer at *People* I felt at home, which was not surprising, considering that it served for a time as a sort of French Foreign Legion for journalists who for one reason or another didn't fit the mainstream media mold. The magazine started as a spin-off of *Time* magazine's "People" section, and when I got there it still covered people of every sort. I wrote about stuff worth writing about: a lynching in Mobile, Alabama; Cambodian immigrants under attack in Revere, Massachusetts; the needlessly fatal crash of a defective school bus in Kentucky. I interviewed beat poet Allen Ginsberg and bellicose pundit Patrick Buchanan, and wrote a cover story (the worst-selling ever) on the death of Yippy leader Abbie Hoffman.

In due course, I accepted a promotion from writer to editor, because that's what you're expected to do, and it's easier and pays more—a tough combination to beat. But *People*, trying to satisfy a readership with a diminishing interest in anything real, had shifted its focus almost exclusively to celebrity stories, and my ideas about what made a good *People* article had diverged from those of my boss, the managing editor. I pitched a piece, for example, on the completion after twenty-nine years of the first stage of New York City's sixty-mile-long Water Tunnel No. 3, the largest public construction project in the city's history. We could run pictures of the gargantuan tube eight hundred feet beneath Park Avenue, I suggested, and interview the surviving daughter of one of the twenty-three workers killed while constructing the tunnel. "Without water, nothing else matters," she'd said at the dedication ceremony.

This was a revelation to me: Without water, there is no life, and without life, *nothing matters*. The rocks and the fire and the sky are inconsequential, make no difference, have no meaning. We have created all the meaning that there is!

This meant nothing to my boss.

My fate was sealed at a meeting when I suggested an article about the two women vying for a U.S. Senate seat from Washington, one liberal, one conservative, each claiming the mantle of typical housewife—a perfect story for our overwhelmingly female readership, I thought.

The managing editor scrunched her nose as though something smelled bad.

"Well, it's not exactly Courteney Cox getting engaged," I conceded, alluding to the most recent of our many cover stories on the *Friends* star. My colleagues around the table *laughed*, and the managing editor evidently felt that the merriment was at her expense. From that moment I found myself in a steel-cage death match with my boss, and I wasn't scripted to win.

I didn't belong there anymore, anyway. The magazine had changed. The world had changed. Nothing stays the same.

With my position at *People* spiraling in ever-tighter circles around the drain, my wife urged me to e-mail Jerry Levin, the CEO of Time Warner, and ask him for a job at corporate headquarters. That would be Jerry Levin, the CEO of a global media and entertainment company—*that* Jerry Levin. *People* magazine was just one of Time Inc.'s more than one hundred titles, albeit the most profitable one by a wide margin, and Time Inc. was just one of eight divisions[3] of Time Warner. To Jerry Levin, I was a point on a speck on a dot on the horizon. For me to ask him for a job would be ridiculous.

"No, you should do it," my wife said. "He *likes* you."

It was true that Levin—either the man himself or the Greater Metropolitan Jerry Levin, comprising "his office" and "his people"—had responded affirmatively to an e-mail I'd sent him

---

3 Time Warner then comprised Time Inc., HBO, Turner Broadcasting, Warner Bros., New Line Cinema, Warner Music, Warner Books and Time Warner Cable. AOL crashed the party in January 2001.

a couple of years earlier asking if the company would pay for a bimonthly lunch where employees could write letters for Amnesty International. But it was ridiculous to think I could work at corporate headquarters. There was nothing I could do there. I didn't have an MBA; I didn't wear a tie.

But women see the world clearly. It's men who are the hopeless romantics. We think we're lone cowboys; we answer only to ourselves; the corridors of convention can't contain us. Women know better. They see what has to be done, and what can be done.

"Say you'd like to help him with his Vision and Values initiative," my wife insisted. "Just try it."

Levin had set in motion a complex and lengthy process, involving hundreds of executives from across the company and innumerable meetings led by high-priced management consultants, aimed at identifying Time Warner's core beliefs and setting them forth in a carefully drafted statement of vision and values.

He'd been inspired by a best-selling business book, *Built to Last: Successful Habits of Visionary Companies,* by James C. Collins and Jerry I. Porras. The authors had studied companies at the top of the corporate heap and concluded that what enabled them to outperform their competitors was a commitment to a vision and a set of core values. (An organization's vision is its basic purpose, its reason for being. Values are the fundamental ideals and beliefs that guide the organization as it pursues its vision.)

At Johnson & Johnson, for example, the company credo was reputedly chiseled in the wall at headquarters: "We believe our first responsibility is to the doctors, nurses and patients, to mothers and fathers and all others who use our products and services." So when someone laced a few Tylenol tablets with cyanide in 1986, the story goes, the CEO took one look at the credo and knew what to do: Johnson & Johnson recalled every bottle of Tylenol nationwide—never mind the expense—and didn't put the brand back on sale until they'd developed tamperproof packaging. Tylenol survived; the company prospered; an example was set. Levin said he wanted Time Warner to be like that—a force for good in the world that people would be proud to work for.

While his Vision and Values effort was under way, Time Warner and America Online announced, in January 2000, their intention to merge, and the idea now was that shared values would help knit the two very different companies together.[4] Once Time Warner decided exactly what its values were, they could be cobbled together with AOL's in a single statement that the senior management and directors on both sides could agree on. There was a lot of work to be done.

I wrote an e-mail to Levin, saying, not in these exact words, "Values is my middle name—I'm *all about* values—and I would be *so* into working on this for you."

I clicked SEND. A minute later, "he" answered me: I should come to corporate headquarters and meet with Don Guerette, vice president, compensation and organization development.

A few days later, I dressed up in hard, relatively shiny black shoes, a suit and a tie, and walked from the Time & Life Building across Sixth Avenue to Time Warner corporate headquarters at 75 Rockefeller Plaza. There I found Guerette, a youthful man in his sixties, clad in sneakers, chinos, no tie—he resembled the real me—who seemed amused and delighted by the idea of my working at Corporate. (Life in general amused and delighted Guerette, but I didn't know that yet.) The next thing you know, I was working with Time Warner's Human Resources and Corporate Communications departments on the company's Vision and Values campaign.

---

4   The combined company, AOL Time Warner, will be "founded on a shared sense of responsibility to the common good," Levin and AOL's chairman and CEO Steve Case declared. In fact, Levin said, "A major basis for our merger with AOL was our shared vision and values."

Wednesday, April 19, 2000

Met with a Time Warner community relations executive to discuss a signature social responsibility project that we could launch right after the merger with AOL closes next January, to help the new AOL Time Warner secure a reputation as a force for good in the world—the sort of force for good that a city would be proud to grant a cable franchise to, or a federal regulatory body wouldn't want to hassle about monopolizing Internet access—that sort of force for good.

The community relations director had a surprisingly huge office. Normally, I expect to meet with people whose offices are about the size of mine—otherwise, why would *I* be meeting with them? I instantly reassessed whom I was talking to, and by the time I traversed the stretch of carpet from door to desk had switched my communications mode to RECEIVE ONLY.

"We've got to do 'Bridge the Digital Divide'; it's a pure winner for AOL," the power-suited woman said with apparent enthusiasm. I nodded in apparent agreement.

For forty minutes I listened respectfully as this well-tailored woman gave me the AOL line: What poor people really need is to cross the Digital Divide—that is, gain Internet access, which will give them a fair shot at jobs in the "digital economy."

When she'd finished laying out the case for our new company to focus its philanthropic efforts on getting Americans online, I agreed to write up some "talking points," so executives wouldn't be struck dumb if asked a question involving bridges and divides. Then, as I stood with my hand on the doorknob, the community relations director addressed me in a completely different, more conversational voice. "I think the Digital Divide is bullshit," she said. "There's a housing divide, an education divide, a food divide. It's a class divide, but we can't talk about class in America." She added that it doesn't matter what we think; in the end, AOL, which is taking us over, will simply tell Time Warner what the social responsibility project is going to be, anyway.

Tuesday, June 13, 2000

I can actually make the case that vision and values are important:
They help attract and retain talented employees. They help unify
the corporation. They help ward off government regulation: fewer
flaws, fewer laws.[5]

They help the company pass social screens of socially responsible investors such as pension funds and universities. They help
maintain an identity for a quickly evolving corporation. Oh, yeah,
and also we actually believe in integrity, respect, and . . . oh, never
mind.

Tuesday, June 20, 2000

I got a raise at *People* when I moved from the hard work of writing
to the somewhat easier work of editing. Now I have moved up the
corporate ladder to headquarters, the point of the pyramid, where I
do a little less and get paid a little more. There seems to be a system
of compensation here, which, if consistently applied, would dictate
that people who ascend to the highest reaches of an organization
could do practically nothing and get paid a fortune, and then, if
relieved of their duties altogether, be handed untold millions as
they walked out the door. But that would be absurd.

Thursday, July 13, 2000

I open an e-mail from a twenty-five-year-old friend at *People:*

> *I got promoted just a few days ago from fact-checker to staff*
> *writer. When I got the promotion, of course I was happy at*
> *first, but then I felt, well, distinctly uncomfortable with the*

---

5 Amitai Etzioni, "Corporate Behavior: Fewer Flaws Mean Fewer Laws," *Business and
Society Review* (1992).

*comfort level in my life. I mean I've been trying to become
a writer ever since I got to* People. *I have always wanted to
write. But recently, it's been weighing very heavily on my mind
that I'm not doing the world any good at this place. That writing here isn't something I find truly worthwhile or rewarding
in any larger sense. I'd like to find outlets through which I can
still write, but at the same time be working for something I can
believe in. I mean, I do volunteer work, but I think I'm looking for a reason to jump out of bed EVERY morning.*

*I really admire the fair and uncompromising way you
live your life and stick to your principles. So, I just wanted to
ask—got any words of wisdom?*

No, not really.

Monday, August 28, 2000

JACOB S. LITTER, PEDDLER, it says on my grandfather's 1897 citizenship certificate, framed on my wall. Now here I am, swimming
at a midtown gym while getting *paid* during my lunch hour, and
I'm not *happy?*

The word *happy* originally meant lucky, smiled upon by fortune, and I'm nothing if not that. My problems—ennui, boredom,
a lack of purpose—these are the kind of problems you want to
have. Real problems, like hunger, thirst, and cold, lie far from my
door. I have everything I need.

I've been reading *The Happiness Myth* by Jennifer Michael
Hecht. She points out that the images of happiness in our fables
and fairy tales are "fantasies of superfluous abundance." The
Promised Land is a land of milk and honey. "We know how you
end up living happily ever after," she says. "You start from too
little to eat." But, Hecht observes, "[T]he fact that the jump out
of poverty gives us a true 'happily ever after' does not mean that

further leaps in food, stuff, and status will do anything like that for us."[6]

So what will?

Sitting on the edge of the pool before I plunge in, I contemplate the undulating reflections of light dancing on the surface of the water. The truth is revealing itself, if only I could comprehend it. The truth is here, right before my eyes, and it's comforting just to sit quietly and look at it, knowing that what I am seeing is what is.

I used to sit at *People* story meetings drifting in and out as other editors discussed Brad and Jen's marrying or splitting up, and I would wonder, "How could anyone possibly be interested in this?" Now I'm sitting in a Time Warner meeting where the chief financial officer is talking about increasing the company's revenue by $500 million in the first post-merger year, and then by a billion, and then by billions more, and I'm wondering, "Why would anyone want to do that?"

Actually, most *People* editors weren't really interested in movie stars, except in a detached, professional, and ironic way. (Everyone understood why I told my mother I worked at the *Journal of Contemporary Biography*.) Celebrity romance and relapse were simply our stock in trade. As for *People* readers, I supposed they were fascinated by celebrities because they cast them as demigods whose lives, loves, and losses play out what our lives could be were we unbound from the fetters of necessity. Take away the need for money, the requirement to be at a workplace, the constraining effects of an imperfect body, the ball and chain of family obligation, and what have you got? A life without limits: Do what you will, be what you wish, go where you please. What would human beings

---

6   As Thoreau put it, "Superfluous wealth can buy superfluities only."

do in such thrilling and dangerous circumstances? Who would we be if we created ourselves? What are we, *really*, when you take away the forms that mold us? Let's watch Icarus soar toward the sun and find out.

Maybe that's why these Time Warner executives want to make our company the richest in the world: so they can become demigods, too.

Friday, September 8, 2000

Twenty-two stories below my office window the ecstatic screams of teenage girls surge and subside, surge and subside, like waves on a demonic sea. Celebrities are arriving for the MTV Video Music Awards at Radio City Music Hall just down the block. Something eternal underlies these oddly melodic eruptions of vital force, yet there must have been a time long ago when there were no celebrities to swoon over. What did girls used to do? Denounce witches? Martyr themselves for the gods? Dance around the fire with their flat bellies glistening in the light?

I have just emerged from a lengthy meeting devoted mainly to batting around my proposed revisions to version six of the ninth draft of AOL Time Warner's Mission and Values. (AOL preferred the word *mission* to Time Warner's *vision*. Whatever.) Somebody suggested we insert three words into the mission statement: "To become the world's most respected and valued company [transforming the future] by connecting, informing and entertaining people everywhere." Norman Pearlstine, the editor in chief of Time Inc., supported the idea.

I disagreed. "I don't think it means anything," I said. "How can you transform the future? You can't transform something that has no form yet." Pearlstine looked pissed.

Afterwards, a more-experienced friend and colleague assured me that the Time Inc. chief's chagrin probably had nothing to do

with what I said; he was just pissed off because he didn't lil
there. "I Ie looks across the table and sees you and me, scr
ink-stained wretches. There was no one else there at his level. He
was too important for the room."

(My friend suggests that the mission statement begin with the
line, "AOL Time Warner: There is no escape." He says that when
he turned fifty, he realized there isn't limitless time, and he wants
to spend it doing something he cares about. "Rather than get used
to things," he says of corporate life, "you find them more and more
intolerable.")

Back at my desk, I got down to work on my Dear Val queries.
Employees have been invited to e-mail questions about the company's Vision and Values to a fictional advice columnist, "Val," and
it's my job to answer them.

"Dear Val," wrote a Turner Broadcasting System employee
concerned about the "synergies" that the company has promised
when we merge with AOL in January 2001. "Are we going to lose
our jobs?"

I sought guidance from my boss on this one. He said I should
just repeat what our CEO has told the press—that the merger
is about growing revenues, not cutting costs. Of course, my boss
added, in an organization of ninety thousand people, you can't
guarantee that *no one* will lose a job—people here at Corporate are
going to lose jobs.

"Well," I said, "the first rule of rhetoric is 'Concede what you
can't deny.' Maybe I should toss in a sentence about how we can't
guarantee no one will lose his or her job?"

"No, just stick to the original line," the boss replied.

I said "Okay" but decided not to answer the question at all
rather than turn Dear Val into one more conduit for bullshit.

It's common knowledge among corporate communications
professionals that employees will give their best efforts to a company that respects them enough to tell them the truth—even when

the truth is that layoffs are coming. I wasn't rebelling against the company. I was actually trying to do my best to preserve, protect, and defend it. Why? Because it's *my job*.

The more I think about my work, the more I feel that I'm not doing what I should be doing. Of course, this feeling is based on two suppositions:

1. There is something I *should* be doing; and

2. I'm not doing it.

As she crawled into bed tonight, Halley, my thirteen-year-old daughter, asked me whether she should change the way she acts, in order to be more popular.

"Be yourself," I said.

"It's hard to be myself, because I'm not sure who I am," she said.

"Welcome to the club," I said.

Monday, September 25, 2000

A Time Warner human resources veteran tells me that our idea of using Vision and Values to build teamwork across AOL and Time Warner—the very enterprise that butters my bread—will come to nothing. Time Warner and AOL occupy different universes. Time Warner's culture is rooted in the Waspy collegiality of Time Inc., the artistic self-regard of Warner Bros., the missionary zeal of Ted Turner and his broadcasting company. We like to think we are carrying on traditions of worthy endeavor, and we try to go about our business with a certain, shall we say, *class*. AOL's culture is grounded in the belief that the Internet *changed everything*, that only AOL people understand how the new world works, and that everyone else should just shut up and let AOL make as much money as possible as quickly as possible, in every possible way. And they own us.

Tuesday, October 3, 2000

In the subway I saw a poster advertising the NYU School of Continuing and Professional Studies. A sun-kissed young woman stands in Central Park, gazing skyward as though contemplating the stratospheric upper limits of her nascent career. I AM THE PRESIDENT OF ME, INC., the poster proclaims.

Good for her!

I wonder if I could get a job like that?

I was in Central Park today, too, walking to work after dropping my son at his school on the Upper West Side. Milkweed seeds were floating ethereally through the air. *That works,* I thought. *So why isn't everything a milkweed?* My business brain kicked in and I realized: It's a *niche product.*

Then I came across an actual niche: a crack in a granite outcropping. A gnarled little evergreen was growing out of it, like those trees you see clinging to the blasted rock face at the side of the highway—life seizing its chance and then hanging on as the eighteen-wheelers blow by. If I were to worship anything, I thought, I could worship this tree.

I turned and hurried off to work.

Saturday, October 21, 2000

I'm scared.

One day when I was six or so, I looked up at my mother standing at the kitchen sink, and I asked her how grown-ups could do what they do every day, knowing they were going to die.

"I just try not to think about it," she said.

She's dead now.

It doesn't even make sense: She is dead. There is no *she*, no *is*.

My father, too, my aunts and uncles—all out of existence. *Poof.* I used to think *passed away* was a euphemism, but it's exactly what happens.

There are boxes in my basement filled with letters and papers and mementos of mine. Now my parents' keepsakes are stacked there, too. Why do I hold on to this stuff? Gravity is inexorably pulling it down, from desktops to drawers to basement to burial in a landfill. Or maybe it will be burned and fall as sooty rain, smearing the windshields of people trying to see.

Friday, October 27, 2000

I saw Time Warner CEO Jerry Levin arriving at work this morning. He got out of an ordinary black car-service Lincoln, alone, schlepping a bag. He looked tired.

I foolishly stuck to my plan of stopping at the newsstand to buy the *New York Times*, instead of seizing the opportunity to hop on an elevator with Levin. I could have told him the Amnesty International lunches he supported were still going strong, or that I think the Time Warner Social Responsibility Statement needs work. Anything. *Yo! Jerry! I exist!* Damn, I'm just not quick and nimble—number two on the list of values AOL posts on its website:

Pioneering
Quick and nimble
Always improving
Consumer-focused
Team-oriented
Integrity
Responsible

I've tried to explain parallel construction to the AOL contingent. (Can you imagine the French storming the Bastille shouting, "Free! Equality! Fraternal!"?) But what can you expect from people who call their personnel directory "People Look-Up"? They sprinkle words around like AOL sign-up discs. "Free 500 hours! [of Internet access] in the first month."

Five hundred hours! I thought when I saw that one. *Why stop there? Why not make it 600 hours—or 700?!* Then I got a disc in the mail: "Free 700 hours in the first month!" In a thirty-day month there are 720 hours. To actually use those 700 free hours on AOL, you'd have to cut down your eating and sleeping to five hours a week. "Integrity" is one of their values. Hah! They're trying to fool you. They want your money.

Duh! Tell us something we don't know.

Okay, but what can I tell you? You can't see much from where I sit. I'm like Jonah in the whale.

Tell us about the whale, Jonah. Give us the inside story, the story behind the headlines.

How the hell am I going to tell you the inside story? I can't see a fucking thing! I'm in the belly of the beast.

Thursday, November 9, 2000

"In the story of Jonah and the Whale," I tell my friend Bruce Frankel, a one-time *People* writer, over lunch at the Time Inc. cafeteria, "Jonah wants to be a prophet, a radical, a revolutionary. He wants to change Nineveh, but God causes him to be swallowed into the belly of the beast. Sort of like me."

"I would assume that being in the whale's belly is a metaphor for the quiescent period of the hero," Bruce replies. "There are many heroic tales in which the hero gives up his crusade and leads a domestic life, but then a new cause arises and he picks up his sword and crusades again."

As if.

Speaking of the belly of the beast reminds me of something I learned in elementary science: Basically, all animals—inchworm, whale, you, me—are a tube within a tube. The key to life is to have food enter one end and come out the other.

ink of it, we could learn a lot from our intestines.
where to begin if I were presented with a piece of
o metabolize the carbohydrates, reduce the poly-
...ues to monounsaturates, and diffuse the nutrients through a
semipermeable membrane into the bloodstream, while maintaining a pH balance of 7.4. I do not understand that process at all. But
our intestines can do all that blindfolded, no hands.

Tuesday, December 5, 2000

At a staff meeting, we discuss the big round of layoffs, as yet offi-
cially unacknowledged, that will be announced shortly after the
AOL Time Warner merger closes in January. A vice president
notes that at Apple, people *expect* layoffs every time there's a merger
or acquisition. "It's an accounting convenience," he says.

"Do the people laid off look at it that way?" I ask.

"It lets the company write off the costs of the layoff as restruc-
turing expenses," he says. "They understand."

Wednesday, December 20, 2000

Bruce Frankel asked me, "Do the bosses even think of the people
they lay off as people, or just as numbers?"

"Well, let me put it this way," I replied, and then quoted the
response I'd written that morning to an employee inquiring about
layoffs: "'As our organization evolves, we will continue to look for
efficiencies, and do what's best for the business.'"

Thursday, December 28, 2000

When Halley or Johnny call me "Dad," I think of the difference
between how I feel on the inside and how they see me from the
outside. I'm just some guy, but to them I am their father. What is

it like to have me for a father? Do I seem to be judging them? Do they feel responsible for my dark moods?

Monday, January 8, 2001

Today I went over my *History of Philanthropy and Innovation at AOL Time Warner*, which I've been working on for months, with the head of Corporate Relations. She told me to write a script for a PowerPoint presentation, to help the leaders of our businesses know more about the new, combined company. "We'll probably want to show it to [President] Dick Parsons and [CEO] Jerry Levin," she said.

Be still my heart! Status. Self-respect. A secure job.

Thursday, January 11, 2001

With approvals from government regulators finally in hand, the deal is closed. Time Warner has been acquired by AOL, and Chairman Steve Case and CEO Jerry Levin make a joint announcement delivering the good news:

> *This is an historic day for the media and communications industry and an exciting time for everyone at our new company. AOL Time Warner is accelerating the transformation of the way people work, play, and communicate. It is our goal* [Reader alert: Here comes our Mission Statement!] *to become nothing short of the world's most respected and valued Company by connecting, informing, and entertaining people around the world in innovative ways that will enrich their lives.*

Case and Levin may really believe that this particular corporate merger will enrich people's lives, but I think they're wrong. I'm inclined to believe that bigness is bad and hugeness is worse, so that the gigantic new company will presumably be a pernicious force, shutting off ideas, homogenizing humanity, and appropriating every means of communication from which profit can be wrung. AOL Time Warner is like The Blob,[7] ever expanding, sucking the life out of everyone and everything in its path, not consciously malevolent, just blindly omnivorous.

Saturday, January 13, 2001

The *Los Angeles Times* publishes an interview with AOL Time Warner co-chief operating officers Dick Parsons and Robert Pittman:

> *Q: What about layoffs?*
>
> *Parsons: This merger is not about layoffs. But in any merger, you are going to have some overlap and some redundancy . . . with the exception of co-COOs (laughter) . . . There will be some reduction initially. But not anything like you see when two banks get together and 10,000 people [are laid off]. There will be some personnel actions you will hear about in the coming days, but nothing material.*

Tuesday, January 23, 2001

Today is the day that we in Human Resources and Corporate Communications have been planning for: Bad News Day. All across the company, 2,400 people are being asked to step into their superiors' offices, where they are told that they're being "let go."

Let go—the phrase intrigues me. It suggests that people have been wanting to go, have been prevented from doing so, and are now being permitted to depart. Either that or they've been held aloft—like trapeze artists, by the wrists—and now they're not going to be held onto anymore.

---

7 I'm alluding, of course, to the 1958 Steve McQueen classic horror film, *The Blob*, about a gelatinous alien life form that consumes everything in its path.

My mentor, Don Guerette, who's seen this sort of slaughter too many times before, stopped by my office at the end of the day. I recounted how everything we've done for the past few weeks has been aimed at achieving a finely tuned, disciplined communications strategy, so that all the layoffs would be announced today and then, boom, tomorrow morning those left standing will get notice of their historic-sounding Founders Grants of stock options, so that they'll scarcely have had time to shed a tear for their fallen comrades before they'll be dancing on the tables.[8]

"Dancing on the caskets," he said, with a sardonic smile. "Good job, Jim."

At a muckraking site called Insider.com, an item entitled INTERNAL AOL TIME WARNER NEWSLETTER RALLIES THE TROOPS BY 'HUMANIZING' LEADERSHIP takes potshots at a story I wrote, ALL TOGETHER, NOW! (I was rather proud of that headline.) The Insider.com writer observes, "The technique is mainly old-fashioned hucksterism, mixed with lessons from management seminars."

I can just picture the angry young man writing these scathing criticisms. He looks a lot like me twenty years ago.

Wednesday, January 24, 2001

A top executive stood in front of everyone in Corporate Human Resources a few weeks ago and assured us that there wouldn't be many layoffs. I remember exactly what he said, as he called for questions from the employees: "I will tell you everything I can. If I don't know, I'll say so. I want to be *as honest as I possibly can.*"

What is that supposed to mean, "as honest as I possibly can"? I wondered at the time. Now I know. He was telling the truth—that

---

8   As it turned out, the merger-day options, giving recipients the right to buy AOL Time Warner stock at $48.96 a share, quickly became worthless, as the share price spiraled downward to levels far, far below that price.

he could not be honest. One hundred of the five hundred employees he was talking to lost their jobs yesterday.

"Twenty-two years," a laid-off receptionist told me through her tears. "This was my first job out of high school."

All of the receptionists, except on the senior management's floor, have been fired. Now when we get off the elevators we'll be greeted not by a human being who knows us but by locked glass doors with electronic ID readers. The savings can be easily calculated, but what about the cost?

My colleague Peter says people used to get mad about layoffs, but now they get sad, as though it were their own fault. They're so indoctrinated with the notion that layoffs are necessary for efficiency, which is necessary for growth, which is the unquestioned ultimate goal—to grow. For what?

I wrote another communiqué from AOL Time Warner CEO Jerry Levin and Chairman Steve Case, to run in the first issue of *Keywords*, the new magazine for employees.[9] By connecting, informing, and entertaining the people of AOL Time Warner, *Keywords*, I said, would help the company achieve its mission of connecting, informing, and entertaining people around the world. And, I concluded, the magazine would help us appreciate that "whatever our division or business, we are all AOL Time Warner people—and proud of it."

There's a certain *integrity* in being a corporate flack. You are what you are, and you needn't suffer the existential tension that comes with purporting to be a journalist when you're really something else. Whenever I start to think I might be better off working at, say, *Time* magazine, all I need to do is glance at the December 17, 2000, *Time* Person of the Year issue, with the picture of the

---

9 I suggested we call it *The AOL Time Warner Company Magazine*, but nobody listens to me.

magazine's two top editors kowtowing to George W. Bush in the White House. In the accompanying text, *Time* managing editor Walter Isaacson shares his thoughts on the 2000 presidential election. "The magic of democracy," Isaacson writes, "is that it sometimes produces the right president for the times."[10]

Wednesday, January 31, 2001

My alienated labor today was to write talking points for executives who may need to speak to employees about the merger. I said it might be a good idea to acknowledge that we all share a sense of excitement and anticipation and maybe some trepidation about what the future holds. My superiors approved only excitement and anticipation.

Why did they cut *trepidation*? Certainly most employees are worried about their jobs, with 2,400 heads rolling down the corridors already.[11] Why not establish some credibility? I don't get it. Maybe what they're concerned about is that every word an executive utters can be picked up and shouted from the rooftops by the financial press? That must be it.

I asked a colleague who knows the ropes if my guess was right: Was *trepidation* struck because business reporters might make a big thing out of it?

"No," he said. "Corporate communications is Politburo speak. Why would employees feel trepidation? Because they might get laid off? We don't do things like that. Everything's good here. We're all happy bees in a happy hive. Happy bees make more honey."

---

10 Magic indeed: Considering that Bush lost the election by 543,895 votes and the Florida recount was going against him, the victory handed to him by five Republican Supreme Court justices was quite a trick.

11 By the end of the year, about 6,200 people had been laid off.

Friday, February 9, 2001

In the hope of escaping corporate communications and getting back into journalism, *any* journalism—it's an imperfect world— I met with Norm Pearlstine, the editor in chief of Time Inc., to seek his help in finding me a job at one of the company's magazines. I had worked as a contributing writer at *Time* for two years between gigs at *People*. Maybe I could make myself useful there, or at *Fortune* or *Sports Illustrated*.

"If you had your druthers, what would you like to do?" Pearlstine asked.

To be honest, I should have said, "You know those engraved collectors' pages the Postal Service puts out with each new commemorative stamp—the ones that explain in a paragraph or two the history and importance of, say, Gettysburg, or the humpback whale, or the bicentennial of Wisconsin? And those pages go straight into albums that people save forever? I'd like to write those pages."[12]

Instead, I said I'd like to be an editor at *Time*, helping with the special series they're putting out: The Best, The Border, and Solutions 2001.

He said he'd keep me in mind.

Friday, February 23, 2001

Today I am writing my first speech for Jerry Levin, brief remarks to be delivered at a tribute to departing CNN anchor Bernard Shaw, who's leaving the network after twenty years—why, I don't know, though I can't help noticing a tilt toward youth among the people on camera at CNN.

This is, in fact, the first speech I have ever written for anyone.

---

12 I wrote the United States Postal Service inquiring about such a job, but got no response.

In search of an apt quote, I read some of the writings of Bernie's namesake George Bernard Shaw, and came across the observation that "The one true hell for a creative person is serving the base ends of self-interested people, and his one clear duty is to rebel against this role."

You talkin' to *me?*

Actually, I'm sure G. B. Shaw's description of hell hits close to home for a lot of my colleagues. A tremendous amount of unhappiness can be ascribed to the fact that so many of us have every aspect of the creative personality except for the creative part. Oh, well.

Monday, February 26, 2001

I struck up a conversation with the Buddha in front of 75 Rock.

His name is Vern. He says he fought in the Filipino forces on the side of the United States during World War II and came to America in 1972 because he hated Marcos. He has no Social Security number because he was never a salaried employee; he had an import-export business. The business failed somehow, so he's on the street asking for money.

Vern is old, thin, and small. Long wisps of white hair straggle off of his bald head. He sits perfectly still, his back to the curb, his eyes open but totally blank, pointed at the sidewalk a few feet in front of him. In his right palm stands a tall paper cup with a few coins at the bottom.

When I put in a dollar bill, he takes it out of the cup and puts it in his pocket. From a marketing standpoint I would think he ought to leave the paper money in there, in order to communicate to his target audience that giving paper money is not unusual but in fact a thoroughly normal thing to do. But he must know what he's doing. Maybe some people look and see paper money and resent his affluence, idleness, and ease. Maybe others hit him and take the money. Perhaps I should discuss this with him and learn something. But to what end? So I can be knowledgeable, worldly, and wise, and think well of myself?

Vern somehow is able to sit like this for hours—motionless except for his shivering on cold days—as a river of midtown businesspeople courses around him.

When I put money in his cup, he looks up into my eyes, smiles—his forehead forming wavy lines like a sandy sea bottom—and nods yes, thank you, yes, you got it right, yes we understand.

As I walked into our building I spotted AOL Time Warner chief operating officer Dick Parsons a few steps ahead of me. I hustled and got on the elevator with him.

"Hello, young man," he said.

"That's nice to hear," I replied. "I'm fifty-two. How long am I young?"

"You've got a good eight to ten years," he said. (Parsons is the same age as I am, but seems older, perhaps because he is a much bigger man, physically and otherwise.)

"I'll make the most of them," I said, as I got out on 22.

"Have a good day," Parsons said.

"Have a *productive* day," I replied, in the grip of some sort of madness. *Thank you* would have sufficed.

"I'll do my best," he said sourly, looking distinctly unamused.

Oh, jeez. I'd overstepped my bounds. It goes: He says something; I reply. He says something; I reply. He says something; STOP. I *know* that. For me to hit the ball again at that point—it's like slapping the queen on the back—*way* out of line. Shit, I just wanted him to remember me.

Which reminds me: I hitchhiked from Provincetown, Massachusetts, to Fairbanks, Alaska, via Los Angeles, when I was twenty. Somewhere around Taos, New Mexico, I was picked up by a Hispanic man in a beat-up old pickup truck. He might have been fifty or sixty; it was hard to tell, his face was so weathered from a hard life in the hot sun. He told me he was going to make a side trip off the highway to visit a woman, and we veered off onto a dirt road that wound behind the hills to a village with chickens running around dirt yards in front of houses that were scarcely more than huts. He went into one of them and after a while came out with a warm Coke for me. Then he drove me back onto the highway and as far along toward Santa Fe as he could.

We'd been together for the better part of an afternoon when he pulled over where our paths diverged. He turned to me and asked what I did for a living. I told him I was in college.

He whooped with joy and slapped my knee. "Any job!" he said. "Any job!"

Then he looked at me quietly, his eyes brimming with tears. "Remember me," he said.

I do. I always have.

Friday, March 2, 2001

I retrieved yesterday's *Daily News* from the trash for the *Lola* comic strip I'd read on the way into work. (It had taken me twenty-four hours to get my head around the idea that *Lola* could have something interesting to say. What next? *Marmaduke?*) Lola is sitting on a park bench surrounded by her scraggly, crazy friends and family, and she's thinking, "My life has interesting characters, but I'm having trouble figuring out the plot."

There it is: Thanks to the destruction of traditional culture and traditional roles, everyone is a writer. We all have to write our lives. And we want our life stories to be *stories*, full of drama and meaning. A corporate communications job at AOL Time Warner doesn't do the trick. Who's winning, Time Warner vs. Disney vs. Viacom vs. News Corp.? Who cares? They're all moral equivalents (well, okay, maybe not News Corp.). What's the point?

Monday, March 5, 2001

I read in *The New Republic* that when Diahann Carroll was making *Julia*, she told *TV Guide*: "Of course! *Of course I'm a sellout. What else would I be? I've sold my talents for a job I'm not particularly crazy about. . . . Isn't that what people do? Isn't that what most people do?*"

Wednesday, May 30, 2001

I felt guilty because I spent ten minutes of the company's time e-mailing the president of Egypt, asking him to grant clemency to a woman sentenced to hang for the murder of her husband. Then I put Amnesty International's Urgent Action notice away and turned to my work—rewriting the options information site on the company intranet.

Thursday, August 2, 2001

Applied weeks ago for jobs in public relations at Oxfam America, Human Rights Watch—and Amnesty International, which has an opening for the position as editor of the organization's magazine. I haven't heard a word from any of them.

Wednesday, August 15, 2001

> *Dear Jim:*
> *As you know, your position at AOL Time Warner Inc. (the "Company") is being eliminated as of January 1, 2002. However, pursuant to the terms and conditions of this letter agreement (the "Agreement"), AOL Time Warner Inc. (the "Company") will provide you with the benefits set forth below . . .*

My boss had warned me this letter would come. "I know when a plate is full," he'd told me, employing a common business-speak metaphor, "and your plate is not full." He meant that I didn't have enough work to keep me busy every minute, so I was a goner in the next round of cost-cutting layoffs. There wouldn't be any lamb's blood on my door post when the death cloud rolled through.

I can't complain. They've given me more than four months' notice—a very respectful and civilized way to part company.

Friday, August 31, 2001

A rail-thin black woman in a wide-brimmed straw hat with a hand-lettered sign on its crown, JESUS LIVES, is evangelizing on our subway car as my son and I head in to school and work, respectively. She delivers her full-throated sermon as a bearded, black-hatted Hasid continues to daven over his Hebrew prayer book a few feet away. (A large man, he had declined to slide over to make room for Johnny and me because, he said, he cannot sit on the seam between two seats.)

The woman concludes her jeremiad: "God put the breath of life in you, and at any time that breath can be withdrawn. So be prepared to meet God! Have a pleasant day."

Tuesday, September 11, 2001

As I walk home from trying to give blood at the Brooklyn Marriott (it turns out there is no one who needs any, no one at all), an envelope flutters down from the sky and lands on the sidewalk near my house, which is across the river from the World Trade Center. Addressed to the IRS in Newark, it's unstamped and empty, neatly singed around the edges and smudged with soot.

Our front steps are covered with a layer of gray ash. My little boy says to me, "The ashes—that's not just the building, you know."

Friday, September 21, 2001

"What's the bagpipes?" I ask my friend Peter.

"They're burying firemen."

I'd like to go down and stand in the street by St. Patrick's Cathedral, to show my respect for the fallen, but I have to stay at my desk and compile a list of all the good deeds AOL Time Warner has done in this crisis.

Friday, October 19, 2001

I just finished a speech for CEO Jerry Levin to deliver in Shanghai. (Of course, I never deal directly with Levin; my boss does that. I'm just given a rundown of the points to cover.) "Carried on with proper sensitivity to each country's law and custom," communications and commerce over the Internet can be a great boon to countries on both sides of the Pacific, I wrote. "Law and custom" is our code for China's system of censorship. We never allude to their custom of putting bullets in the backs of people's heads. Seldom have I engaged in—what's the word? Corruption? Collaboration?—so directly.

"I can't in good conscience write this stuff anymore," I deadpanned to a colleague. "I'm going to resign." He laughed appreciatively. What effect would my gesture have on AOL Time Warner? On China? Anyway, maybe it's better to engage with the Chinese rather than isolate them.

It works for me.

Sunday, October 21, 2001

Prior to September 11th, my friends and I were schlepping along. Now, we are doing exactly the same things we were doing before, but it's "carrying on." We were ironically detached, and bored. Now we are serious people, and determined. Presto. And just bringing home the bacon and hugging the kids seems enough, more than enough. Life is not absurd when someone's trying to kill you.

Friday, November 2, 2001

On a brilliantly crisp and clear fall morning, walking up 51st Street to work, I am greeted by wailing bagpipes again, knots of firemen on the sidewalk, yet another funeral. The bagpipes say, "Be grateful you're alive; be grateful you're alive to make a list of cross-company *Harry Potter* promotions after kissing your family good-bye this morning"; or do they say, "Be grateful you're alive. Do not squander your life making a list of cross-company *Harry Potter* promotions"; or do they say, "It's not about you, Jim."

Firefighters from departments all over the country come to the funerals to show solidarity with the New York firefighters who died on September 11th.

I wonder whether corporate communications people from other companies would come to the funerals if AOL Time Warner Corporate Communications got blown up.

Friday, November 9, 2001

This morning, I look out my office window and see a tremendous evergreen tree lying prostrate in Rockefeller Plaza, a crane towering over it, and little men in bright red coats swarming around it like ants on a dead bird.

They've cut down this beautiful tree! What were they *thinking?* This magnificent tree survived bitter winters, blazing droughts, windstorms, lightning, bugs, blight. It survived everything but Christmas.

Slowly the crane pulls the tree upright. Amputated, it sways helplessly a few inches above the ground. Does it feel its phantom roots? A captive giant dwarfed by the granite towers hemming it in on all sides, it looks bewildered. Its boughs writhe in the wind.

Friday, November 16, 2001

As I sit reflecting upon the passage of another week of my life, I receive this e-mail:

> *Subject: People Solutions 2001 Conference*

> *Dear Mr. Kunen:*
>
> *In today's customer-driven world, the value your people create increasingly drives the financial results your business delivers. The People Solutions 2001 Conference, sponsored by Towers Perrin, explores this issue. . . .*

Do I live in a customer-driven world? Must I?

I'm not interested in People Solutions. But shouldn't I be? Businesspeople make the world. Without businesspeople, I wouldn't have this phone, this computer, this table, this electric light, this shirt on my back. I would be shivering, hungry in the dark. And I want my stocks to go up, don't I? All right, then, let's go, you people who create value and drive results. Please, keep it up.

Still, these mailings touting corporate communications conferences where I can learn how to drive my company's message, get buy-in, lift morale, use the latest social-networking tools—I find them enormously depressing. While I keep my head down at my desk, I'm fine. I derive some satisfaction from writing well, or editing poor writing into clear English—what I call defending the language—or bantering with a few colleagues whose company I enjoy. And then something like this conference invitation ruins it all, by reminding me what I'm doing.

Thursday, November 29, 2001

Never mind. My boss tells me I'm not going to be laid off in January. He didn't explain why. I assume they've wrangled a bigger budget, or somebody else is leaving, or something. Don't ask questions.

Wednesday, December 5, 2001

CEO Jerry Levin, whose vision led Time Warner into its ill-fated union with AOL, and whose values, whatever else they were worth, failed to keep our stock price from plummeting, announces that he is retiring. He says he wants to do "something that is socially significant but also creative."[13]

Don't we all.

Wednesday, March 13, 2002

"Did you ever in your wildest dreams imagine that one day you'd be an apologist for the ruling class?" my boss said to me.

I just smiled. Nothing I could say would do me any good.

Hearing of my boss's remark, my eleven-year-old son, Johnny, said, "Well, you probably never imagined you'd have two kids and go to yoga classes on Thursday nights, either."

Thursday, March 21, 2002

Riding the F train to work, I suddenly realize what would be the perfect job for me: casting director for a movie, *Subway Goddesses*. "You," I would say, "and you, and you." I would select women of

---

13 After leaving Time Warner, Levin got divorced, married a New Age psychotherapist, and together with her started a high-end treatment and optimal-performance center in California, Moonview Sanctuary, where fees start at $2,500 for a half-day, $5,000 for a full day, minimum $15,000.

he female life force in all its heartbreaking forms. I

would they play in the movie? What would the story be?

I don't know—something about love and loss, courage and kindness. Hey, I'm just the casting director.

Tuesday, April 2, 2002

Did my annual interview with CEO Dick Parsons for *Keywords*.

"You're comfortable," I said, deploying a euphemism we both understood to mean rich beyond the wildest dreams of avarice. "So why be the CEO? Who needs the hassle?"

"That's a really good question," he replied, "particularly in today's world, when people are beginning to look at work-life balance issues. Why work? In reflecting on it you realize that you have to do something with yourself from the time you get up in the morning to the time you go to bed at night. So the next inquiry would be, 'What would I find interesting, and rewarding, and maybe somewhat useful from a larger perspective?' And the net of it is that as I thought about those questions, I thought that what I was doing at the time, being president of Time Warner, scored higher on those three metrics than anything else I could think of—and so too about this [CEO] job.

"I've never known what I want to be when I grow up," Parsons continued, in his typically charming and disarming way. "The one word that I would use: I want to be *relevant*. I want to count for something, be relevant to the way the world unfolds—and this is a terrific platform from which to operate."

Soul mates! *Relevant* was what we college students used to demand that our studies (and by extension, ourselves) should be, back in the sixties, when Dick and I were young. And he'd found a way.

Wednesday, April 10, 2002

A couple of weeks ago, in the Rockefeller Center concourse, I stumbled into an orchid show, a weird menagerie of delicate and dangerous-looking things of every shape, size, and color, with nothing in common save their ineffable orchidness. Today, in the same place, I encountered an exhibition of classic motorcycles— exuberantly shining steel, another kind of beauty. Or is there only one kind?

Monday, July 15, 2002

Out my window I see an endless array of rectangles: rectangular windows in rectangular buildings on rectangular blocks. My computer, my desk, the cabinets, the heating vent, the little door on the vent you reach through to try to adjust the temperature—everything rectangular. There is no roundness in my life at work.

I read in today's *Times* that the NYPD is trying to harden likely targets for terrorist attack—for example, the Empire State Building and Rockefeller Center, where I remain at my post, undeterred, courageously promoting and defending the imperial Corporation.

Wednesday, July 24, 2002

Dick Parsons, who succeeded Jerry Levin as AOL Time Warner CEO in May, announces that the Securities and Exchange Commission has launched an investigation into AOL's accounting practices in 2000 and 2001.

In light of this news, my boss decides to take our Mission and Values off of the company's website. He's concerned that the press will mock us for proclaiming our commitment to Integrity and Responsibility (though no one could doubt AOL's dedication to

Agility, which could serve as a thieves' credo: "We move quickly—embracing change and seizing new opportunities.").

I'd have thought if we really believed in our values, we would stand by them, *especially* when we're under attack. But perhaps it's just as well. Maybe adherence to ethical conduct really should go without saying. Every company's statement rehashes the same things, anyway: We will maintain the highest ethical standards, make quality products, treat our employees with respect, and so on. As opposed to what? We will maintain fair to middling ethical standards, make shoddy products, and treat our employees like old shoes?

Friday, October 18, 2002

I'm in Charlotte, North Carolina, to write a "Diary of a Company Man" column for *Keywords*, the company magazine, about AOL Time Warner's giving a computer and free Internet access to each family that moves into a new home built by Habitat for Humanity here. The good news is that this enables a few kids to do their homework. The bad news is that we've been so good at insinuating our technology into the schools that teachers now assign homework requiring Internet access and frown upon handwritten papers. We've managed to disadvantage the disadvantaged.

That a lucky handful of Habitat kids can now get on the Internet at home is indeed a blessing, because they can't stay for after-school computer time, because they have to get on the buses home, because court-ordered busing requires them to travel across town to school, because the city's housing is almost completely segregated (as it is everywhere, let's be fair). So, the kids can now sit at home online, where, as isolated individuals, they can live in a state of constant yearning, which makes them into perfect consumers, whose needs can be created and fulfilled by advertising and e-commerce on the Internet. The Internet is both the problem and the solution! Brilliant.

Updated '60s rallying cry: IF YOU'RE PART OF THE SOLUTION, YOU'RE PART OF THE PROBLEM.

Thursday, October 24, 2002

"Sure, whatever you want," my colleague Peter said this morning, when I walked into his office to ask if I could turn down the heat. (The control for our group of offices is on his turf.) Peter is completely amenable to my (unavailing) efforts to get comfortable in my office. This is a perfect example of something that's wonderful because it could so easily be horrible—if he insisted on some brutal heat setting, for instance, or even if he locked his office door when he was out.

"Are you familiar with Simone Weil?" Peter asked. I ventured a guess that she wrote *The Second Sex.* "No, that's Simone de Beauvoir," he said gently. "Simone Weil was a Jewish mystic who became a Catholic and hung out with Dietrich Bonhoeffer. He died in a concentration camp and she died of pneumonia in the Resistance."

The Resistance! Now there was a reason to get out of bed in the morning.

"Okay," I said. "What about them?"

"They came to believe that Christianity was impossible if you had the Church," Peter said. "In my old age I'm coming to believe the same thing." The Church, in Peter's view, has become a power-based hierarchy and bureaucracy like any other organization, and is thus antithetical to Christianity. The whole New Testament, Peter says, is about love versus power.

Peter went on to tell me about the time that, as a young Vista volunteer in the South Bronx, he stood waiting for a bus and looked up at the tenement windows and thought about all the human lives unfolding inside without making a ripple in an indifferent universe, passing away to nothing. Then the bus came, and as he got on he was suffused with the knowledge that Jesus is the living Christ, present at all times and places. Peter became at that instant a Believer, and remains one to this day.

"You've got to tell me where that bus is," I said.

"It's everywhere," he said. "It's everywhere and it's nowhere."

Friday, October 25, 2002

Spent much of today writing my weekly quota of *Way to go!* notes for CEO Dick Parsons to send to people around the company. Once in a great while, Dick actually orders one up; occasionally, HR or PR people in the divisions suggest the lucky recipients; most of the time, I find them myself by combing through newspaper clips looking for executives who've boosted profits or Time Warner cable installers who've snatched drowning toddlers from backyard pools, making the company look good. I judiciously exercise this awesome power to thank, because the CEO actually reads and signs the notes. He becomes aware of the existence of the people I anoint, and then, *anything could happen.*

A Warner Music Group PR exec recently wrote, "I have gotten such great feedback on the notes that Dick has sent out to some of our key artists recently, it got me thinking about how you might expand that program internally."

Can you imagine Jewel (whom I/Dick recently commended) raving on the phone to—to whom? A friend? Does she have friends? Her agent? "You wouldn't believe the thank-you note I got from Dick Parsons today! I swear, I don't care what they offer, I'm signing with Warner Music Group again."

I wish I could tell my parents. It took me a full year after my bar mitzvah to write all the thank-you notes, and my glacial pace

was a source of considerable tension between me and
who was fielding calls from people asking whether t
had been lost in the mail.

The thing was, it didn't feel right to just dash off a note saying
"Thanks for the great gift." I wanted to craft a brief essay about each
particular present, how ingenious it was, how perfectly suited to
me, how eagerly I anticipated using and enjoying it.

Jump ahead forty years (or forty-one, depending on whether
you count from the beginning or end of my bar mitzvah thank-you
note writing), and here I am, the Designated Thanker for the CEO
of the world's leading media and entertainment company—and
you've got to figure he'd have the best. So, that was time well spent,
at thirteen, lying on the bedroom floor, laboring over those notes.
Even then he knew. Only, I didn't know. You never know.

Friday, November 1, 2002

Every second Thursday, after I've been drawing down my bank
account for two weeks, I find it completely replenished. Time
Warner calls it direct deposit; I call it the Miracle of the Loaves.
Every time it happens, I'm suffused with a feeling of well-being
that lasts for several hours.

Friday, November 8, 2002

Summer, fall, winter, spring. Summer, fall, winter, spring. If only I
could slow down this relentless succession. I don't even bother to
switch from screens to storm windows in the back door anymore,
because you just have to switch them right back. I've settled on a
permanent compromise—top panel: screen; bottom panel: storm
window—so it's always more or less okay. Could be better, could
be worse.

Monday, November 11, 2002

When I told my colleague Peter Ainslie the other day that I'd made no attempt to translate a jargon-filled piece about AOL's latest tech toys into plain English, because it was obviously aimed at "young people," I noticed that the tonal quote marks I put around the words are fading. As we get older, the gentle self-mocking irony wears away, and the phrase means what it means.

Wednesday, November 13, 2002

I talked with Don Logan, longtime president of Time Inc., recently drafted by Parsons to head up the newly organized Media and Communications Group, which includes the rapidly deflating AOL. Logan, unlike the other top executives I've spoken with, seems to really be there when you talk with him. You don't get the feeling that you're facing a Wizard-of-Oz facade; you're talking to the actual man, and he's actually listening to you. This may account for Logan's enduring popularity with the people who have worked for him over the years.

I ask him a lot of things for the company magazine, and one thing for me: Why does everybody talk about growth all the time? Why can't we just go about our business doing what we like to do and making a nice profit every year?

"You have to grow," he said, "because if you're not growing, you're standing still, and pretty soon you're moving in the other direction, and the other guy will eat your lunch."

This called to mind an enduring memory. When I was a freshman in high school, my science teacher beckoned us over to a microscope and said, "Look at this." I took my brief turn and saw two single-celled creatures trying (if you can use the word *trying*) to envelop and consume each other. It was a fight to the death. Maybe you can take that as your model and build from there, if you want to understand the world; or at least that's one way to understand it.

Thursday, April 24, 2003

At an off-site meeting for a legion of PR executives from all of AOL Time Warner's divisions, CEO Dick Parsons squeezed my shoulder and shook my hand as he passed my table—in full view of all the others, whose shoulders he did not squeeze, whose hands he did not shake. I basked in the glow of his attention—as though he were my father, or everybody's father.

It was my job to interview Don Logan and Jeff Bewkes, Entertainment and Networks Group chairman, in front of the assembled PR people. I got a laugh when, in reference to my son Johnny's disinclination to be the only teen in America not downloading pirated music from the Internet, I explained, "We have a saying in my family: 'If you can't be a saint, don't be a chump.'"

Jeff Bewkes responded, "We have a saying in my family, too: 'It's not enough that we win; others must lose.'"

Interesting.

The Bewkes family's saying got me thinking: What would happen if, when introduced to musical chairs in kindergarten, a child said, "I have an idea—let's get another chair?" Or if, safely seated, she got up and offered her place to the kid left standing? What would become of such a person?

Thursday, May 29, 2003

In the midst of a Pilates class at the gym, I was overcome by vivid memories of my father and my mother, who died a decade ago, and I missed them terribly. Tears welled up in my eyes. It's been too long since I've seen them, and it's only going to get longer.

Tuesday, July 22, 2003

Epic thunder and lightning as torrential rain sweeps over the funeral procession of Cuban singing legend Celia Cruz, the Queen of Salsa, at St. Patrick's Cathedral down the block. The throngs *cheer her casket* as it goes by.

Wednesday, December 10, 2003

"How many people do you see sleeping down here that have a nice soft bed at home?" shouts the bearded man in filthy clothes who lectures subway passengers in the 53rd Street station. "If they had a bed, they'd sleep in it! Same with people who say there's a better life in heaven. If they really believed there was a better life in heaven, they'd go to it! It's all bullshit!" Then he starts talking about how this is not really a democracy; this is a police state; democracy is bullshit. He thinks everything is bullshit.

Monday, January 5, 2004

Time Warner Center, with one-third more floor space than the Empire State Building, is like a mountain, but it's also like a wristwatch: It's a complex mechanism that runs. More precisely, people run it.

Shortly before we moved our corporate headquarters from Rockefeller Center, Ed Cavanaugh gave me a tour of the insides of the new building, the areas white-collar types seldom see. As director of operations, he oversees the heating, ventilation, and air-conditioning; the water and the fire-safety standpipes and sprinklers; the electricity and emergency backup generators—the respiratory, circulatory, and nervous systems that keep the building and its occupants alive.

In a sub-concourse somewhere deep beneath the ground, we hiked a disorienting series of long, *long* passageways to a steel catwalk overlooking four 15,000-gallon water tanks. *This looks like a James Bond set*, I thought.

Then we took an elevator to a cramped, windowless office where I marveled at the automated building management system that maintains temperature and air quality and who knows what else, monitoring the building's vital signs in a welter of graphs and diagrams on an array of screens. *This looks like the bridge of the* Starship Enterprise, I thought.

Nearby, I saw the air-conditioning system's three chiller plants— each utilizing a pair of cylinders the size of small submarines—which pump refrigerant and water through huge pipes festooned with pressure gauges and big, red iron valves. It looked like *Twenty Thousand Leagues Under the Sea* to me.

I turned to images from fiction to get my head around what I saw because in my real life, I don't encounter these realities. I don't see behind the wallboard or above the ceiling or beneath the floor. It was a humbling experience to look at the pipes, ductwork, and wiring that run through those places. No wonder they're hidden from sight; it would be disheartening to be confronted by these things every day and be constantly reminded that you have absolutely no idea how things work and could never fix anything if it broke. Such helplessness! This is the secret shame so many of us feel each time we face a plumber or electrician or cardiologist: *My life depends on you. Please be kind.*

Fortunately, Cavanaugh did not hold my ignorance, ineptitude, and manifest uselessness against me. He displayed the generosity of spirit that comes with knowing what you do and why you do it: People need light and people need heat and people absolutely need water.

The amazing thing is that I'm quite certain I get paid more than the operations workers who keep the building going, the workers upon whom everything else depends, the workers the company could not do without, even for a day. Why? Because I have "higher-order skills" that are bid up in the marketplace? I doubt it. I suspect I get paid more because the fix is in. The executives with their hands on the money dole it out with a finger on the scale for people like themselves—because they can, and by doing so they solidify their station in life. People like us will pay people like us more than our fair share; we can count on it. We don't even give it a thought. It's just the way things are.

Friday, February 6, 2004

In the wake of one of those pointless organizational reorganizations that strikes us from time to time, a couple of our colleagues have decamped to another department on a different floor, and I've been offered the opportunity to move from my one-window office into one of their two-window offices. Of course, I would have to be insane not to make the move. (Status is so firmly attached to square footage that one woman counted the ceiling tiles in each of two apparently identical offices in order to take the one that was larger, albeit imperceptibly so.) But I *like* my office. My neighbors are quiet, and there's no telling who or what might move in beside me if I relocate. What to do?

"Take the big office," my younger and wiser friend Stephanie advised me. "You'll feel better about yourself."

[I did, and I do.]

Monday, November 22, 2004

The latest in my continuing series of unpublished letters to the editor of the *New York Times*:

> *To the Editor:*
> *I was struck by Bob Herbert's choice of words as he wrote movingly of our country's scandalous inattention to the problems of the poor ("Shh, Don't Say 'Poverty,'" Op-Ed,*

November 22). "*We are surrounded by poor and low-income people,*" Mr. Herbert wrote.

I wondered, what is this group called "we," and when were the poor kicked out of it?

Rather than lament the fact that "we" are "surrounded" by these unfortunate others, I would state the fact this way: "Many of us are poor and low-income people." If our problem were viewed this way, we might give it some of the attention it deserves.

Tuesday, December 21, 2004

During lunch hour I ran into a friend of mine from Brooklyn on West 58th Street. I pointed out the new Hearst Building under construction down the block from Time Warner Center. "It's a really interesting building," I said, pointing out its unique facade of stainless-steel triangles and sloping glass.

"Not like this thing," he said contemptuously, gesturing toward Time Warner Center. "It reminds me of Houston."

I've never been to Houston, but it was clear that the comparison was not intended as a compliment. I took offense. I felt insulted. Oh my God, I'm identifying with the corporation. This is my *home.*

I'm free-falling through time, or time is in free fall.

It's hard to maintain a sense of the size and shape, the weight and depth of your life. It's a blur of daily-ness. At Time Warner, day follows day week after week, month in and month out. I work hard. I'm super busy. I get paid.

Monday, April 4, 2005

Visiting the set of *Friends* (a Warner Bros. production) on display at Time Warner Center, I sit on the Central Perk coffee shop's orangey-brown tufted sofa, the one that Chandler, Ross, Rachel, Phoebe, Monica, and Joey sit on at the end of the opening titles. How thrilling is this? Jennifer Aniston sat here. She was here; I am here; we are connected. We are in precisely the same spot; only the time is different—and time, what is *that*, exactly? So here we are, Jennifer and me. I am definitely feeling something. It could be a stray electron shed by Jennifer, or just the pure concept, the idea, the memory—the memories we share. Remember that sofa on the Central Perk set, Jennifer? I do.

Wednesday, October 5, 2005

Tucked inside a folder in the Time Inc. Archives is a carbon copy of a press release entitled "*Fortune* at a Glance"—flawlessly typed, each letter stamped into the page by the force of a secretary's deft hand: "Time Inc. has announced, for publication in January 1930, a deluxe monthly magazine. Its subject is Business . . . The magazine's name is *Fortune* since it deals with the factors which control the fortunes of every man."

Time Inc. archivist Bill Hooper says that the company, concerned about the cost of maintaining the archives, may just scan the documents into a computer and discard the originals. He believes that the materials should be preserved. So do I.

It's one thing to read in a history of Time Inc. that the articles in *Fortune*'s first issue included "a discussion of the economics of orchid growing."[14] It is quite another to open a folio, turn

---

14 *Time Inc.: The Intimate History of a Publishing Enterprise, 1923–1941*, by Robert T. Elson, p. 143.

the magazine's creamy vellum pages, and encounter, in a full-page photo with the luminous delicacy of a watercolor, a single white, purple, pink, and yellow flower, moist and alive in a green glass vase.

I look closely at the first-issue cover (*Fortune, February 1930, One Dollar a Copy—Ten Dollars a Year*) printed in bronze and black on stock as thick as cardboard. A bare-breasted goddess lounges atop a horn of plenty, beside her wheel, her hand resting lightly on a spoke as she gazes heedlessly off into the distance. Behind her, men labor at a port, carrying sacks from ships, driving freight-laden wagons, hewing stones, laying foundations— busying themselves with the business of their lives, despite the fact, or maybe because of the fact, that at any moment the wheel may turn.

Thursday, May 25, 2006

Yet another in my continuing series of unpublished letters to the editor of the *Times*:

> *To the Editor:*
> *Re: "Of Love and Money," by David Brooks (column, May 25)*
> *I had thought that Social Darwinism had long ago been rejected by even the most unrepentant apologists for an inequitable status quo. But then, in my ignorance, I had also thought that the widening income chasm between rich and poor might be caused by factors such as the reduction in taxes on dividends and capital gains on the one hand, and the erosion of the minimum wage, on the other. Thanks to David Brooks, I now understand that income inequality is in large part attributable to the "good brain functions" that tots of the higher social classes develop, thanks to the*

superior, stable, loving relationships they enjoy with their upscale parents.

I am grateful for having the roots of wealth and poverty so clearly explained, but I remain perplexed by one question: Why does Brooks describe himself as "a scientific imbecile"?

Tuesday, August 15, 2006

I put on a telephone headset, sit down beside a Time Warner Cable customer service representative, and listen in for several hours as she handles an unending stream of calls.

Remind me to tell you about our money-saving phone service. My name is Natasha. How can I help you?

Her recorded greeting affords Natasha Smith a few seconds to breathe before handling the next incoming call. She is halfway through her 1:00 p.m.-to-midnight shift.

"I'm having trouble with my modem," an exhausted-sounding customer says.

"I am sorry for that," Smith says sympathetically. She asks the caller to unplug the Ethernet wire from the router and plug it directly into the computer. "Now unplug the power to the modem and then plug it back in and restart your computer." Smith surfs through a succession of screens with headings like MAC ADDRESS SEARCH RESULTS and MODEM RESET COMMAND ACTIVATED, dancing through windows inside windows, now and then typing data into colored boxes, then observes, "I can see that your signal is going through."

"Yes, the computer is working now," the woman says, relieved.

"Thank you for allowing me to help you today," Smith concludes. "Have a good evening."

Remind me to tell you about our money-saving phone service. My name is Natasha. How can I help you?

Dressed comfortably in blue jeans and a sleeveless gray top, Smith sits at the end of a row of attached workstations separated by sound-dampening panels. Her place is designated by two signs, one in red type, NATASHA SMITH, #1289, and one in black, DESK NO. 1140J DO NOT REMOVE. On her desktop sit a computer, a phone, and a silver, heart-shaped picture frame holding a photo of her and a smiling baby boy.

Smith is one of 461 customer service representatives at Time Warner Cable of New York City's Flushing Call Center, and I'm here to show that the company values each and every one of them. Working in two large rooms in a low-rise brick office building in Queens, they take 25,000 to 35,000 calls per day. They strive to handle each in an average of 315 seconds, their voices blending into a mellifluous babble that rises and falls like waves against a distant shore.

My name is Natasha. How can I help you?

When she takes her 7:00 p.m. lunch break, I ask Smith, a recent graduate of Long Island University with a degree in computer science, where she learned to be so patient and polite.

"From my mother," she says. "She's a home health aide who takes care of elderly people, twenty-four hours a day. That takes a lot of patience.

"Some people call, they're upset, but if you talk to them in a certain tone, like you're eager to help and you want to get their problem resolved, at least 99 percent of the time they turn around and they're okay, they're calm," she continues. "Ever since I got this job I'm nicer to people now, when I have to call up some kind of company. I'm much more nice, because the shoe's on the other foot. I know how it can be."

I ask her what she likes best about the job.

"That it's a job," she says.

Wednesday, January 10, 2007

The Arab American Association of New York has accepted me as a volunteer. I'll be helping immigrant teenagers to write better in English.

I picture myself working with an Arab teenager—he might be named Ahmed or something like that. I'm counting on Ahmed to be someone I care about, and to be responsive to my efforts to care about him. Our relationship should develop over time, so that there will be some sort of narrative arc to carry me forward, get me out of bed in the a.m.

The way I see it, or foresee it, the story of Ahmed and me could unfold in a few basic ways:

Ahmed will start out mistrusting me, and I will gradually overcome his mistrust, and he and I will develop a wonderful mentor/mentee relationship, only to have his anti-Semitic parents step in and forbid him to see me anymore. I will then go to see the parents, who will relent, and we will all have demonstrated how age-old enmities can be overcome by the power of love.

Or, I will go and see the hostile parents, who will not relent, and thus we will see how individuals are overwhelmed by historic forces larger than themselves.

It's also possible that his parents won't sense that I am a Jew, or won't care, and will be delighted by our wonderful mentoring relationship, given the great progress Ahmed is making in school. Then again, our mentoring relationship may not be so wonderful, and Ahmed may not make much progress in school—and in any case, his parents may never be aware of me at all. What then?

I'm not even sure that Ahmed is an actual Arab name. Perhaps I will learn that it's not, and that will be just the first, small step I take on a path that leads to unimagined discoveries, leading to the surprising conclusion that, though I went to teach, it is I, in fact, who have learned something important—though I can't imagine what that could possibly be. I mean, there is an endless amount of information I could acquire—or reacquire—including the enormous number of things I have known at one time or another. But as far as grand insights go?

Where I live in Brooklyn, I see Arabs every day. Some of the older women keep their hair and entire bodies, but not their faces, covered by black cloth. Some of the younger women wear head scarves (hijabs), but otherwise dress as Westerners. I remember once I saw a little Arab girl in running shoes and jeans chewing gum and singing a then-popular Madonna song, and it gave me goose bumps—the Americanization of Shoshanna, or whatever an Arab girl's name is. Her parents might be horrified, but that's the way it goes. You think I understand Yiddish? Ask me anything about baseball, though.

Anyway, here's my plan for teaching the Arab kids:

To begin, I will ask them to tell me and one another about themselves. Then, surprise, I will point out that they have *selected* information they think is important, and they have *ordered* it in a way that helps the listener follow. I'll tell them that this is what they must do when they write—that the most important decision in writing is *what goes in and what stays out*, and the second most important is *in what order*.

For homework, I will ask them to write a brief description of themselves.

In class the following week, I will ask them to interview one another and then write a description of the person they interviewed.

Eventually, we will move to reporting—they will interview somebody and write a story.

Somewhere along the line I will tell them, "Something for the ear, something for the eye," and perhaps read this sentence from page 778 of *Swann's Way*: ". . . across from him, in a pink silk dress with a long string of pearls around her neck, sat a young woman who was eating the last of a tangerine."

Wednesday, January 31, 2007

First night at the AAA. Walked briskly from work to 57th and 7th, down the stairs for the N train. An R train comes through; a W train; another R train. Finally, an N train. Switch to the R at 59th to Bay Ridge Avenue in Brooklyn. Takes exactly one hour.

I find the storefront doctor's office that harbors the Arab American Association at 6:30 and go in. There's nobody in the front room. The door to the back room is locked. *Hello!* I call. *Hello!* No one responds. I dial the association's number on my cell. The phone at the reception desk right in front of me rings. I could answer it myself. No one else does.

Finally, Heidi, the young AmeriCorps staffer who awarded me this gig, comes down the stairs and lets me in. Three kids told her they'd come, but no one has shown up. We wait. We talk. No one comes. We'll try again next week.

Wednesday, February 7, 2007

Half a dozen Arab American teenagers show up, emphasis on the American. They speak English fine, and are at my session because their parents are involved with the AAA and think it would be a good idea. The kids don't think it's such a good idea. I spend an hour mostly trying to maintain order. I have learned something important: I'd rather teach adults.

Wednesday, May 16, 2007:

Nine kids came to the Arab American Association tonight, an unusually strong turn-out. Without explaining why, I took them on a stroll around the block. As we were walking, I suddenly raised my hands and clapped once, loudly. Back upstairs, I asked the students if I'd done anything unusual.

"You clapped your hands," a seventh-grader said.

"When?" I asked.

"While we were walking outside," she replied.

"That's right," I said, and then we discussed how the past continuous tense ("were walking"), is used to describe the long action that was going on when something happened; and the simple past tense ("clapped") is used to describe what happened while the long action was going on.

The little girl nodded thoughtfully. "They taught us that at school," she said, "*but I never understood it before.*"

I heard angels sing.

Subway . . . work . . . subway . . . home . . . errands . . . subway . . . work . . . subway . . .

Wednesday, November 14, 2007

I've been teaching at the Arab American Association on Wednesday nights all year. The kids' writing class gave way this fall to English lessons for adults with wildly varying needs. One night I had a retired Egyptian military judge who spoke English quite well; a Pakistani teenager who knew no English at all and was illiterate in his own language; and three other men spaced along the continuum between them. What's more, I never face the same class twice. People come and go, drop in, drop out, drop in again. The only constant is Saad.

Saad Atwah, a stout, bald Egyptian in his fifties, was a water vendor in Cairo. Now he stands on a Manhattan street corner six days a week selling hot dogs from a cart so that his son can go to college and become a doctor—which he no doubt will.

One night, as happened fairly often, Saad was the only one to show up. Greeting me as always with a hearty handshake, big smile, and the salutation, "Mr. Jim! Very good!" he handed me a little booklet of one hundred questions and answers for the U.S. citizenship test and motioned for me to begin reading.

"Name three rights that the First Amendment guarantees," I read.

"Speech, religion, press," Saad responded crisply.

"What are the three branches of government?"

"Legislative, executive . . . joo, joo . . ." Saad shook his head and picked up his pencil, my signal to pronounce the word slowly, *joo-dish-ul*, so he could write it out phonetically in Arabic characters.

"How many members are there in the House of Representatives?"

"Washington."

"Where is the capitol of the United States?"

"Four hundred thirty-five."

Saad sometimes mismatched the questions and answers, but we've kept at it for three months, and now he can nail all one hundred, in any order, almost every time.

Tuesday, January 8, 2008

As I walked up Broadway back to work from my lunchtime swim, I saw a MetroCard fall from the back pocket of a young woman walking toward me.

"Miss, Miss!" I said, but she didn't look my way. "Miss," I insisted, raising my black-gloved palm directly in front of her face, "you dropped your MetroCard."

"Oh, thank you," she said, as she hurried back to pick it up. "It's my monthly!" She'd paid $74 for thirty days of unlimited transit rides, a sum that she could ill afford to lose.

It was a nice feeling, being of help, and as I thought about it, it occurred to me that this was the most useful thing I had done during work all week, no, all month—maybe ever.

Later, as I trudged home from the F train after another day of toil, a few steps behind me a man said to a woman, "Your life is flying in front of your eyes because your days are so busy you don't have time to do anything."

Were truer words ever spoken? Somehow, I have now spent *eight years* at Time Warner Corporate Communications.

Wednesday, January 16, 2008

When the day came for Saad to take the citizenship test, the immigration officer never posed a single one of the questions we'd practiced. Saad didn't get that far, because when the examiner began by asking a couple of questions not on the list, probably something like "Where do you live?" or "When did you arrive in the United States?" Saad was unable to respond. He had learned to recognize a hundred questions phonetically and to articulate the sounds of their answers, but he did not speak English.

Wednesday, February 6, 2008

Time Warner released its earnings report for 2007 this morning—the first report under new CEO Jeff Bewkes. (Dick Parsons retired as of January 1.) I dialed in to Bewkes's conference call with business reporters and Wall Street analysts just in time to hear the tail end of his saying something about cutting costs at corporate headquarters.

I went down the hall for coffee and asked my friend Stephanie what he'd said. "He's going to cut corporate costs by fifteen percent," she said. "We just got a memo."

Back at my desk I opened the e-mail, which said that one hundred of the five hundred employees at Corporate were being laid off. Those selected would be treated with "professionalism and respect," it said.

My buddy from Risk Management walked by my office. "Any sign of the Grim Reaper in your area?" he asked with a sardonic smile.

"No," I said. "They want to keep us in suspense. It's more fun this way."

Then I got the phone call. I heard the cheerful voice of Tisha, my boss's assistant. "He would like to see you at 1:00."

"Okay. I'll come to his office."

"No," she said. "He's going to come to your office."

I called my friend Terry—the CEO's speechwriter, who's the only other person my age in the office.[15] "I got one too," he said. "Mine's at one-thirty. It could only mean one thing."

I didn't feel particularly angry about losing my job. It was bound to happen sometime. But I felt nervous about the upcoming unpleasantness of the meeting with my boss, and I noticed I'd lost my normal connection to time and space—that first awareness of strangeness signaling the onset of nausea, faintness, or a bad trip (or all three).

At precisely 1:00, the boss came into my office and sat down, looking remarkably pallid. "This is very hard," he began. "You're a great guy, and you've done a great job. But I had to cut my department budget twenty-five percent, and there was no way to do it without cutting *Keywords*, and your job is *Keywords*."

Actually, my job included a lot of other things, but I said nothing. What was there to say?

"You can feel pissed-off if you want," he suggested.

I sat silently for a few moments, choosing my words. "I think I'll take some time to decide what my reaction is," I replied, in even tones. Only two days later did it occur to me that I should have said, "I don't need your permission to feel pissed-off."

---

15 Four out of the five people laid off in Corporate Communications were over forty.

He told me I should speak with some mumbled name I'd never heard of at Human Resources. I asked him how you spell her name. He didn't know, and he didn't know her phone number, either.

I thanked him. (*Thanked* him?) He stood up. I stood up. I wondered if he would extend his hand to me. He didn't. I stuck out my hand to him. He gave me his, and I shook it.

I didn't call HR. Fuck them. If someone in HR wanted to see me they could damn well call me.

My first thought was to do the top thing on my to-do list—write the e-mail promoting the next issue of *Keywords*—try to shove it over the finish line—but then I thought, *I'm not working for them anymore.*

I walked down the hall to see Terry. He actually looked pale, despite being a dark-complected African American.

"[The boss] told me, 'You can feel pissed-off if you want to,'" I said.

"He told me that too," Terry said. "I guess they've got a script."

We compared what he had said to each of us; it matched up nearly word for word.

I dropped in on Stephanie, who, being young, capable, and lower paid than I, would now have the privilege of doing, in addition to her own work, any duties of mine that did not disappear with me.

"The way they've handled this lets us all know just how much respect they have for any of us," she said. "Where's the memo that says we appreciate the contributions of these people?" She looked sad and angry. (She and two others in the department quit a couple of months later.)

Around 3:30 the ambitious forty-year-old who'd climbed his way into a spot between my real boss and me on the org chart came in and lowered himself heavily into one of the two rarely occupied chairs facing my desk. This fellow acted the part of a nice guy and actually was a nice guy, to a depth of about an inch and a half, until you got to the place where his soul had once been. Right now he looked haggard, with dark circles under his eyes and a green cast to his complexion. His neatly trimmed hair was a little mussed, his starched white shirt a little wrinkled, his tie maybe just a little askew. "This sucks," he said.

"Yeah, I know, it's hard," I said sympathetically. I'd heard many times how difficult it is to fire people. "But as for me, it's okay. I didn't expect to be given a gold watch at this place when I'm sixty-seven years old."

He only stayed a minute.

Around 4:00, a small, dour-looking young woman in a dark blouse appeared in my doorway—the unknown representative from HR. (I suspected that she'd parachuted in for the day from some Firings R Us consulting firm.) "I've been sitting at my desk waiting for you to call me," she said, sounding annoyed and offended, as though I'd stood her up for a date.

"Why would I call you?" I replied. "My boss didn't know how to spell your name and he didn't give me your phone number."

"Well, anyway," she said, and sat down and put a white three-ring binder on my desk facing me.

She opened the binder and said they were offering me a "generous" package. "I'll do my best to read upside down," she continued, pointing out each number with her pen as I leaned forward to see.

They were going to keep paying me for six months—a little more than one week for every year I'd worked there—and they gave me a lump sum, too. I don't really know why they give you anything—so you won't slam the door on the way out? But somehow the word *generous* doesn't ring true, not when they're throwing you under the bus, no matter what package they toss out after you.

Then, halfway down the page, she read that I was being credited with "eighteen years of service."

"That's totally unacceptable!" The words burst out of me, and I recoiled back into my chair as though shoved. "I've been here twenty years! You're not counting my two years at *Time* magazine."

(A decade earlier I'd held the position of "contributing writer" for two years at *Time* magazine. I was one of a number of people Time Inc. called "independent contractors" and didn't provide any benefits to. The federal Department of Labor alleged that we might in fact be employees entitled to benefits, and Time Inc. settled the matter, without any finding of fault. Now the company was not giving me credit for those two years. With them, I'd have twenty years of service and could get affordable retiree medical coverage for my family. Without those two years, we'd be on our own. "Screw you," the company was saying. "Oh, and by the way, screw your family, too.")

"I'll make a note that you don't agree with the years of service," the HR woman said flatly, and wrote something down. "At five o'clock, your computer access will be terminated and your ID will be turned off."

"What! Are you kidding?!" I'd lose my computer and the freedom to get in and out of the building in *ten minutes*.

"If you had come up to my office at 1:30, then you would have had time to close things out properly," the young woman sniped.

"Excuse me," I said. "That's really not the point." I was speaking very slowly and very quietly. "It's not like after twenty years, two and a half hours would be fine."

"You can shoot the messenger," she said.

"I am not shooting the messenger," I said, staring daggers into her eyes. "I have not said one word attacking you, or denigrating you. I have not raised my voice."

"Well, it was your tone," she said. "Maybe I took your tone wrong because I have a sinus infection today and I'm really not feeling well."

Great, now it's all about you, I thought.

She told me that I should clean out my office over the next day or two—it had twenty years' worth of books and files and framed pictures—and she left.

It was five minutes to 5:00. I shot off a succinct memo to my main contacts at Time Inc., Warner Bros., New Line, HBO, AOL and Time Warner Cable ("I'm told my computer is being turned off in two minutes, so I'll be brief..."), typed an out-of-office e-mail message ("My job has been eliminated as of February 6 . . ."), left a new greeting on my voice mail ("Hello, you've reached Jim Kunen at Time Warner. Actually, I don't work at Time Warner anymore . . ."), and sent an urgent e-mail to my boss asking him to preserve my computer access for a day. And then I went home.

Thursday, February 7, 2008

On the subway in to work—or, I should say, to my former workplace—I read in the *Times* business section that Time Warner CEO Jeff Bewkes had taken steps to "eliminate the bloat" at corporate headquarters, cutting one hundred jobs, which he said would save $50 million. *Bloat?* I'd seen that word used in reference to other people at other companies, even in reference to anticipated cost cutting at Time Warner, but now *me?* For the first time I felt the word's vicious sting.

In response to the layoffs, the stock price had leapt 31 cents (2 percent!), from $15.40 to $15.71.[16]

---

16 One month later, on March 6, the share price had fallen back to $14.93. To put this in perspective: On January 7, 2000, the last day of trading before the planned merger with AOL was announced, Time Warner shares closed at $65. Time Warner shareholders got 1.5 shares of AOL Time Warner for each Time Warner share they held, so the holder of 100 shares of Time Warner, who had $6,500 worth of stock on January 7, 2000, had 150 shares worth $2,239.50 on March 6, 2008—a loss of 66 percent. Thousands of Time Warner employees took it in the neck twice, seeing their 401(k) retirement accounts decimated, and getting laid off in cost-cutting moves designed—unsuccessfully—to get the stock price back up. Needless to say, most of the executives who oversaw the merger bailed out of AOL Time Warner stock before it went into the toilet, while assuring everyone else that the company's future was bright.

I scampered up the Columbus Circle subway station stairs—the same long, steep flights I had faced each weekday morning for years, feeling like Willy Loman lugging his sample cases. Today I didn't feel like Willy Loman. I felt like I was nineteen. A whole new life lay ahead of me, waiting to be discovered.

As I walked into Time Warner Center, I recalled the time, when we'd first moved into the building, that my boss asked me what I thought of the cavernous, geometrically stark lobby fashioned of black stone and steel. "I liked it better before they took Lenin's body away," I said. He laughed, then quickly stifled his laughter, reestablishing his distance.

I placed my ID on the card reader at the turnstile. Nothing happened. Dead. Just then, the head of HR arrived. "I'm sorry yesterday was such a hard day for you, Jim," she said. (*Hard day*—another interesting locution. Words fail us.) "Here, I'll get you in." She walked me through the guest gate.

My computer was on, but I couldn't get into my e-mail or my files: NO ACCESS came up on the screen. So, that was my boss's response to my urgent request not to lock me out.

Terry, my speechwriter friend, was packing up boxes in his office down the hall.

"Did you notice the *Times* story says they're cutting a hundred jobs to save fifty million dollars?" I asked. "That comes to five hundred thousand dollars a job."

"That must be *your* salary," Terry said.

Maybe they're counting in dog dollars.

I set about packing or tossing the only evidence of my having worked for the past twenty years. I'd filled an entire small dumpster when I broke for lunch, asking my assistant to leave a pass for me at the lobby security desk, so I could get back in.

After lunch I went over to the guard and said, "I'm Jim Kunen. There's a pass for me." He picked up the phone. "Mr. Kunen is here," he said, and sat silently as the seconds ticked slowly away; he appeared to be on hold.

"I don't think you need to call," I said. "The pass should be in the computer."

"It is," he said, "but there's a note for me to call someone." He held for a few more moments, then said, "Mr. Cockell is coming down to see you."

Oh, Jesus. What now? Larry Cockell was the head of Time Warner security.

I sat on one of the little upholstered benches set in cubbies along the lobby wall and tried to read my *Times*. In a minute, Larry appeared, rock-solid in his gray suit, and sat down facing me, so close that I could peer into the deep furrows of his brow and smell the dryness of his mouth. This was probably not his first tough conversation of the day.

"A person, or a couple of people, called Security to say that you were walking the halls, and it made them uncomfortable to see you walking around," he said. "They were concerned that you were a disgruntled employee."

I took a deep breath. "Larry," I said, "I'm not a disgruntled employee. I haven't said boo to anyone. I haven't complained. I haven't said any swear words. I'm just packing up my office."

"I understand that," he said patiently, "but you don't work here anymore. Now you're just a member of the public, and you can't walk into the building unaccompanied."

"Members of the public don't have to be accompanied," I said. "You just call down and leave a pass for them."

"I know," he said, "but some people were uncomfortable with you walking around the halls."

"Larry, the only place I've walked is from my office to the give-away table to put out some of my books."

"Look, Jim," he said with a conciliatory smile, "you and I go way back. We've known each other a long time. We've had some laughs."

I couldn't actually remember having any laughs with Larry, though I'd worked with him from time to time, and once spoke with him privately to request his support for the Time Warner Center security guards' so-far unavailing efforts to unionize. I'd always thought it was cool to know him—not least because he'd headed President Clinton's Secret Service detail and probably knew five ways to kill me with his bare hands. But I had the feeling now that he wasn't really listening to me; he was running through his talk-him-down hostage-negotiation protocol while assessing my threat factors.

I had come in to work yesterday as a well-respected longtime member of the Time Warner team, and in a heartbeat I'd become an Enemy of the State. I was caught in an exquisite bind. I had to show Larry that I wasn't angry, and that made me *extremely* angry.

To demonstrate that I was not a disgruntled employee, I explained that I was really okay with losing the job—I didn't want to spend the rest of my life at Time Warner—but I did confide that I was pretty unhappy with the ritual humiliation of being treated like a criminal.

"I think you're taking this a lot better than I would," Cockell concluded. He accompanied me up to my office, demonstrating to any onlookers that I had his stamp of approval—or maybe just making sure that's where I went.

Then the next harassment began. An officious former colleague, taking it upon herself to play the role of company dick, popped into my office every few minutes, saying, "Do you need any help? Let me get you some help. How's it coming? I'll send someone down to help you."

"Thanks very much," I said, the first three times. "I appreciate the offer, but I have to sort through what I'm tossing and what I'm keeping. I have to do that by myself." By the fourth time she came by I desperately wanted to shout out loud what I was thinking: "Get the fuck out of my office!" But that would have sounded disgruntled.

Later, I did ask an assistant to come down and tag the art on the walls while I finished the last bits of packing. "I love your NRA Sharpshooter certificate," she said. "How do you get one of those?"

"Go to summer camp," I said. I was gratified that she'd noticed it. I'd hung it alongside my certificate of membership in the District of Columbia Bar to make a statement: Guns or lawyers, I'm your man.

Finally, I called my firer from HR to ask her if my out-of-office e-mail message would keep working for a while.

"What's it say?" she asked.

"'My job has been eliminated as of February sixth. If you need assistance with Time Warner business, please contact Doris Barchi. Thanks.'"

"You should change 'My job has been eliminated' to 'I no longer work at Time Warner,'" she said.

Why do they always have to hide the truth? I guess it's just a habit.

I wrote our office manager a note reminding her that I still had the wrought-iron desk lamp she'd loaned me when we first moved into the building. "If you want it, it's on the desk in . . ." I was about to say "my office," but instead typed "in 15-202."

I turned off the lights and soaked up the view of Central Park for the last time. I looked across at our building's north tower, where through the tinted glass I could clearly see a dozen men in suits seated around a conference table, not going anywhere.

Friday, February 8, 2008

They had reassigned my deputy editor months ago, and then took away my assistant. I was working on weekends and holidays to get *Keywords* out. They had made it harder and harder to do my job, and just when I really couldn't do it anymore, the job ended. Thank

God, now I don't have to write a Company Man column this weekend. And on Monday, I won't need to find out whether *Gossip Girls* won the Publicists Guild Award.

III. Notes from Under the Bus

I wished to live deliberately . . . and not, when I came to die, discover that I had not lived.

—Henry David Thoreau

Thursday, February 14, 2008

I've been downsized. Thrown under the bus. Kicked to the curb. *Killed*, some people call it. This has never happened to me before.

What a rip-off! I made a deal with the Corporation—"I'll do this bullshit job in exchange for money and health insurance to keep my family safe"—and now they're not holding up their end of the bargain: *We don't want you anymore. Get lost!*

But, surprise, now I am found. I had *thought* I didn't like spending my precious days on Earth sealed into a box at Time Warner Center, but I had *no idea.* I wasn't fully conscious of how alienated I was, how estranged from myself. I couldn't afford to be, because then how could I have climbed those subway stairs every morning and kept doing my job?

As is common among white-collar workers, I had fallen victim to a sort of Stockholm syndrome: The more frenetically I worked for my corporate masters, the more justified (or, as shrinks used to say, *well-adjusted*) I felt. I was confident that I was doing what serious people are supposed to do. Everyone around me seemed to feel the same way. The standard response to the question "How are you?" was "Crazed." Only now that I've been let go (released!!) do I realize how true that answer was.

Now I'm free! Anything is possible.

But some things are necessary—like paying the bills. Last year Time Inc. laid off my wife, radio journalist Lisa Karlin. She'd given them seventeen years of limitless labor, work without boundaries—days, nights, weekends (what weekends?), vacations cut short or not taken. (She was ahead of her time in that regard.) "I keep thinking I'll come home and find my career waiting for me on the stoop," Lisa says. "I picture it as a sort of apparition, and it says, 'Don't worry, Lisa. I'm here to rescue you.'"

Fortunately, between our savings and severance, we can view this crisis as an opportunity—for a while, anyway. Lisa's enrolled in social work school, aiming to work with special-needs kids.[17] I, too, would like to find work I care about—a meaningful job, something that subtracts a little pain from or adds a little comfort to the world.

My first job out of college fit that description. As a child-care worker for the Massachusetts Department of Youth Services, I worked in a co-ed group home for a dozen teenagers—Campbell Cottage, it was called. They had run afoul of the law in minor ways—joyriding in stolen cars, smoking marijuana, shooting out porch lights—or had simply defied their parents and teachers so incorrigibly that they'd earned official classification as PINS—Person In Need of Supervision. That supervision was provided for the most part by persons scarcely older than they, such as me. I liked the kids, and the kids liked me enough to help out with our mimeographed newspaper, *The Cottage Cheese*. I enjoyed my coworkers, who shared an interest in being kind to people in need of kindness, in trying to understand people who felt misunderstood, in guiding people who were lost.

I learned some things about raising kids (reflect their emotions, set limits), a bit about stealing cars, and a lot about how little you can do to shape someone else's life. Kids ran away from the program; kids completed the program and got in trouble again anyway; kids who had alcoholic parents when they arrived had alcoholic parents when they left.

But here's the thing: One glorious January day—the earth pure white, the sky a thrilling blue—we took our charges sledding on a hillside in the country. The crystalline air amplified every sound—the squeak of our footsteps on the snow, the shrieks and laughter of the innocent-again kids as they roared down the slope. *Geronimo-o-o-o-o!*

---

17 Update: She got her master's and is now working in a special education school.

That evening I was eagerly telling my friend Joyce Petronec all about the day. (I used to talk about my work back then.) As I described the joyful rides the kids had taken, the clever things they'd said, I interrupted myself: "Of course, I don't know how sledding is going to help them not steal cars in the future."

"Well," she said, "you gave them a good day, didn't you? How many of those does a person have?"

Helping kids have a good day now and then—that could have been a worthy career, but I realized within a couple of years that I didn't want to be a $100 a week[18] child-care worker for the rest of my life. (I didn't want to be *anything* for the rest of my life. Life was much too long for that.) It wouldn't have occurred to me to go to graduate school and get a degree in psychology or social work so that I could run a therapeutic program or programs or a department or a system and really make an impact (and decent money). Anything that came after something that you had to do first did not appeal to me at the time.

So I set sail for New York City (where else?) and worked for several years as a freelance journalist—tossing little pebbles of truth into the national pond, as I saw it—until I yearned to come in from the cold and become part of something larger than myself. I resolved to get a job on a newspaper, and when I couldn't do that (recession, hiring freeze), I went to law school and became a defense attorney at the Public Defender Service in Washington, D.C.

At PDS, my clients were fairly typical of what people think of when they think of criminal defendants. They weren't corporate executives who scammed investors with bogus balance sheets, or banking buccaneers who lured people into loans they couldn't repay. They were poor people in the inner city, and those who were guilty had committed crimes in the street, because they didn't have any better place to commit them. I enjoyed the saintly feeling of

18 $540 in 2011 dollars.

standing with the reviled and friendless, the intensity of counseling people in crisis, the challenge of pitting my wits against the massed forces of the state, the cine-romantic drama of the courtroom, the meaningfulness of defending liberty by making the state prove its case before putting *anyone* (THIS MEANS YOU) in prison. And I was pretty good at it.

But the law was not my calling—as I should have realized back in law school, when I was working as an investigator for the criminal defense attorney who was my mentor. In one of our cases we were defending a twenty-year-old I'll call Izzy, who had been identified (or misidentified) as one of two Hasidic youths who whipped sawed-off shotguns from under their black coats and relieved a camera importer of a brown paper bag containing $10,000 in cash. We were going to make the case that Izzy was being scapegoated because of his reputation in the Hasidic community as a rebel who behaved outrageously, going to movies and driving around in cars.

I was having a glass of coffee at Izzy's family's small walk-up apartment in Brooklyn one night during my winter of investigation, when his father came in, stomping the snow from his galoshes. He extended a great, meaty hand to shake mine. He was a watch repairman, and I wondered how he did that fine work with such big hands. His black overcoat and black lamb's wool hat framed a face as white as paper. Izzy's father had a potbelly, big ears, and a large nose, but he was an exceptionally handsome man, owing to the strength and harmony of his features, the clarity of his eyes, the calmness of his bearing. He was a concentration camp survivor.

"If you could find out what the true story is," Izzy's father said to me, "I would give you such a good present."

"We'll probably never find out what the true story is," I replied, "but I do think that we can get Izzy acquitted—that's the main thing."

"Not for me," the old man said. "For me the main thing is to find out what the true story is."

Me, too, an unheeded voice whispered at the back of my mind.

As an attorney, my job was to build one side of a story and knock down the other. That's the advocacy system. I was proud of my work, and never more so than when I convinced a jury that—based solely on the evidence—up was down and black was white. But my heart's desire was to look at all sides and try to find and tell the truth.

I went back to journalism. Some years later, while toiling as an Op-Ed editor at *Newsday* on Long Island, I got a phone call from John Saar, a reporter I'd met in Saigon during the Vietnam War. (I was over there writing some stories for *True—The Man's Magazine*.) Saar invited me to join his crew at *People*, which is where, some years later, I was sinking when I grabbed a rope and clambered aboard Time Warner Corporate Communications.

One thing leads to another.

Sunday, May 4, 2008

The initial rush of euphoria at being released from the company's yoke dissipated with my first painful premium payment for the aptly named COBRA[19] health insurance coverage. It's lethally expensive, and, what's worse, it doesn't last forever. Soon my family will be at the mercy of the insurance market. That's why for the past couple of months I've spent countless hours and all-too-countable thousands of dollars trying, with the help (?) of a high-priced lawyer, to get Time Warner to give me retiree medical benefits.

The lawyer's theory was that even if they didn't *have* to give me credit for my two years at *Time* magazine, Time Warner would choose to do so if we offered them a rationale to "hang their hat on"; we just needed to give them cover, a plausible reason to do the

---

19 The Consolidated Omnibus Budget Reconciliation Act (COBRA) of 1986 mandated that laid-off employees be able to continue their coverage under their employer's group health plan for a limited time by paying 102 percent of the premium.

right thing. They're not going to shit on two people who've between them faithfully served the company for thirty-seven years. They're not that heartless.

Oh yes they are. Or maybe they really would *like* to help my family out, but they're afraid that if they give me credit for "independent contractor" years, they'll have to do the same for other similarly situated people. How many other people are in my position, with an arguable claim to twenty years of service, I don't know. Three? Five? The cost of providing retirement medical benefits to this cohort could not possibly move the needle for a corporation with $6.5 billion in pretax profits,[20] but okay, first it's one thing, then another; if you start making business decisions based on sob-sister considerations like "loyalty" and "decency," the next thing you know, your expenses are up, your profits are down, and you have no choice but to—what? Let me see. I've got it—lay people off! I would be more sympathetic to this line of reasoning if the CEO didn't go right on getting paid as much as three hundred ordinary employees. The belt-tightening always goes on around other people's necks.

When Time Warner, to my dismay, would not toss me a crumb for old times' sake, I thought maybe they'd do it to avoid getting sued for age discrimination. I knew firsthand how paranoid management could be at the slightest hint of vulnerability on that score. Company lawyers went over every line in *Keywords*, removing anything that could remotely suggest any age-related bias. They were completely maniacal in this regard. In one *Keywords* interview, Time Warner's chief security officer Larry Cockell recalled that thirty years ago, when he was a patrolman in St. Louis, the chief of police put him in an undercover unit, "all fairly young officers—a kind of Mod Squad," Cockell said. The lawyers made me change "young officers" to "new officers." Don't ask. Beats me.

---

20 For 2007, announced on the day I was laid off.

Laying out my case to a lawyer specializing in age discrimination suits, I pointed out that while 50 percent of Time Warner Corporate Communications employees were over forty years old, 80 percent of those laid off were. "If the selection of the five individuals laid off in Corp. Comm. cannot be attributed to their performance, or to their skill sets' suddenly no longer fitting the twenty-three remaining jobs, it is fair to conclude that those laid off were selected on some other basis," I wrote. "The marked tilt toward older employees suggests that age was the real reason for the selections." Made sense to me.

"Does the thirty-two-year-old now doing your work get paid less than you did?" the lawyer asked me.

"Yes, of course she does," I replied. I thought that was the whole point of knocking off older workers, and one reason it's prohibited.

"It's permissible for a company to lay off older people *to save money*," the attorney explained. "That's not age discrimination. It's age discrimination only if they lay you off simply because of your age."

I see. In other words, it's illegal to discriminate against older employees *unless they've been doing good work for your company for many years*, in which case they'll have earned raises, and you can fire away!

Case closed. Now what?

Saturday, May 17, 2008

My entire subway car is covered with advertisements seeking applicants for jobs at New York City's Children's Services agency. In 2006 the city was gripped with sadness and remorse after a beautiful little girl was beaten to death by her mother and stepfather, both of whom had a well-documented history of child abuse. Now we're not going to let that happen again.

ARE YOU COOL ENOUGH TO BE A CHILD PROTECTIVE SPECIAL-IST? one sign asks, over the picture of a young woman who, I've got to say, does look very cool. ARE YOU STRONG ENOUGH? asks another, over the picture of a determined young woman—another actual Child Protective Specialist. ARE YOU WISE ENOUGH? demands a third.

Hell, yes.

"What do you notice about the people in all those pictures?" my wife says, when I share my interest in this useful new career. "They're all young."

I'm *too old?* That's new.

I want another adventure (okay, maybe not one where you walk up and down tenement stairs all day and have to remember a lot of names). I want another chapter in my life. But what can I do? Who would hire me? What are other laid-off people my age doing?

Friday, June 6, 2008

I hoped I might find some answers at Lee Hecht Harrison, an out-placement firm whose services Time Warner and other big companies purchase for shit-canned employees as part of their severance packages. (Why companies spend money to help their former employees find other jobs, I don't know. It could be that surviving executives have a there-but-for-the-grace-of-God-go-I desire to maintain a safety net for the day when their time comes around; or it could be an effort to distract and occupy laid-off workers, channeling their energy into job-seeking instead of revenge-seeking.)

In the Met Life Building (which will always be the Pan Am Building to me), high above Grand Central Station, a Lee Hecht Harrison receptionist—*they* still have them—directs me to a conference room with a jaw-dropping view of Park Avenue stretching to the north. At the table sit seventeen anxious and exhausted people in evident need of orientation. Three of them appear to be about my age; the rest are young.

We introduce ourselves: three UBS investment managers; a structured-finance guy laid off by Bear Stearns and then by Merrill Lynch; a man from structured finance at Standard & Poor's (*What is structured finance?* I'm wondering); a woman and a man from the IT department at Morgan Stanley. Here I am among the walking wounded from the decimated ranks of imperial Wall Street's once-mighty armies.

"There is a lot of activity out there," Karen, a Lee Hecht Harrison career coach, assures us. "A lot of people are landing."

Landing. It seems just the right word for what we job-seekers are seeking. The dazed, sad people around the table look like shipwreck survivors who've clambered aboard a lifeboat and are just realizing they are not saved, but rather destined to drift on the boundless sea awaiting a rescue that may never come. We have nothing in common except the fact that we are all in the same boat—which is a lot in common, come to think of it.

Of course it's important to assess the job opportunities that are out there, Karen tells us. But first, we have to assess ourselves. It's time to do a values inventory. We turn to page 67 in *Book "A,"* *Managing Your Search Project—Part One*, where we are to rank ten values (service, friendship, security, wealth, power . . .) in order of their importance to us.

"When I started out, I was single. I had no children, so security was at the bottom of my list," says Tony, who just got laid off after twenty years at a recently imploded investment bank. "Now my situation is completely different. Security is the top concern." Thomas, who's barely thirty, says he put security at number one, too.

"I notice that security is very important now for people of all ages," Karen observes. "It used to be that the young chose power and wealth, and the older people picked security. Now, all ages want security. Everybody is affected by the volatility."

Volatility. The word suggests a random natural condition— *Increasing volatility will bring thickening clouds and a chance of layoffs*

Friday—as though people weren't making decisions to throw other people out of work.

"Step back," says our coach. "Decide where you are and where you want to go. You get to move forward and do more of what you like to do and less of what you don't like to do. If you've had a job that was stressful or unpleasant, this is your chance to find something better."

She asks each of us to tell the group what we liked best about our jobs, and what we were good at.

Most people say they were good at structured finance, and liked it.

"I don't know what I do best. I want to find out," says Harry, a fifty-something IT guy with slicked-back black hair. "After twelve and a half years in IT, I want to do something socially useful."

See? I'm not the only one.

"I'd been kind of hoping I'd be laid off," Harry told me later. "But the way they did it bothered me." He needed two more months to qualify for retiree medical benefits, and if the company had given him credit for service while he remained on the payroll for severance, he would have qualified. He asked, but they said if they did it for him, they'd have to do it for a lot of people. (God forbid.)

Now Harry was thinking of getting into web development. He was also considering getting a degree in global affairs and finding a job with the UN. Then there was his blue-sky idea: "An ice-cream shop, a coffee shop—it's the people thing that attracts me, send them away happy. But then there's the risk. I could be down the road six or eight months and find it wasn't working. I'm scared shitless. How can I find my true calling?"

A lot of us seem to have the idea that someone or something is out there calling, but very quietly, or at too great a distance to hear. Or maybe the call comes when we are busy, and our minds don't have call waiting, and we don't pick up.

"I want my next job to be different," Harry said. "I've got one more good youthful chapter in my life."

"Well, all you want is something meaningful," I said. "That shouldn't be too much to ask."

Friday, June 13, 2008

Today I saw Enrique, who with his weathered face and white beard looks like Ernest Hemingway. He sits by the entrance to the lot where I park my car, and I pay him to open the gate for me. We always chat briefly, though I can't always make out what he's talking about. He lacks teeth, slurs his words, and makes references to events and people that I know nothing about. Talking to Enrique is like tuning into a program already in progress, always a very lively program, filled with laughter or rage, a given day or hour's emotion depending on—what? Who knows?

Finally, after many 90-degree days, Enrique had shed the heavy parka we gave him last winter. Now he was wearing a T-shirt, blue bandana, and chinos rolled up to the knees. He nodded toward his right shin; a quarter-size wound glistened there, the raw flesh oozing. He laughed and said something about some guy up the street having done something. I couldn't quite understand. Maybe someone kicked him? He laughed repeatedly as he told the story. As I looked at the wound my stomach turned and I had to look away.

I like the *idea* of homeless outreach work, but I don't do well with horrific odors and running sores and bare feet with grotesque black nails. I quickly handed Enrique a dollar, but wouldn't have wanted to help him into a vehicle and ride with him in his barefoot and urine-soaked condition. I don't have what it takes to work with homeless street people every day.

After another session at Lee Hecht Harrison and a swim at the gym, I walked by the loading docks of the Time & Life Building. Men were throwing bookcases and desks into the crusher at the back of a big yellow garbage truck from Fortune Interior Dismantling Corp. One desk bore a large label that read PEOPLE IMAGING ROOM 3743. There go some more jobs. Even the desks are eliminated, into Fortune's dustbin.

Monday, June 23, 2008

I often awake now remembering vivid dreams about losing my job.

I WENT FOUR WEEKS IN A ROW TO CHURCH WITH MY BOSS TO SCORE POINTS SO I COULD GET MY JOB BACK—AS ASSISTANT MANAGING EDITOR OF A MAGAZINE. THEN I THOUGHT, "I'M NOT CATHOLIC. I'M NOT SUPPOSED TO GO TO CHURCH," SO I DIDN'T TODAY.

Tuesday, July 15, 2008

You don't need an education degree to teach in private schools, so I've been applying for every job advertised for English teachers. Maybe I could teach writing? Zero responses. I figured that one line on my résumé, "New York Association of Black Journalists, First Place in Features, 1996," if misunderstood in the right way, might pique the interest of employers in the market for a little diversity. Could it be working *against* me?

Friday, August 1, 2008

As I write this, Gabriel Fluke is lying in the small, malodorous room he shares with two other wasted men in a nursing home for poor people, three blocks from my nice house. During a heat wave a few weeks ago, he collapsed while begging on the street, opening a gash in his head, and soon after that he had a heart attack, and now he's developed pneumonia. He is keenly alert, entirely himself, his sense of humor intact. He has all his faculties. What he doesn't have is money. He's not healthy, not wealthy—and not wise? Who's to say? All I know is that the desire to keep my family out of the situation Gabriel is in is what kept me working at an otherwise pointless job for as long as the corporation would have me.

In the beginning, Gabriel was just one of the neighborhood street people to me—the one who looked like Abraham Lincoln, if Lincoln had lived to become old, sick, and poor: those cheekbones; the deep-set, soulful eyes; the tousled salt-and-pepper hair; the vein standing out above his temple. I'd give him a few bucks when he was begging outside the neighborhood supermarket. Gradually he won me over with his puns and jokes and his solicitous inquiries about my children, whose every change and challenge he photographically remembered.

Soon I was visiting his fourth-floor walk-up hovel, notebook in hand, avidly writing down his tales about his youthful wanderings through Asia and the drug-drenched precincts of Andy Warhol's New York. After a while, I stopped bringing my notebook and started just seeing him because I wanted to see him. And every time I'd emerge from the dark, fetid cave of his apartment back into the brilliant, busy, humdrum world of affluent Brooklyn, I'd look at the hip web-sters with their cell phones and tattoos, the proud young parents pushing high-end strollers down Court Street, and I'd think, *You don't know what you're missing.*

Once, as I puzzled over one of the beautiful, erotic, hallucinogenic pastels he draws—a quasi-human figure in motion against a writhing background of birds and snake-like creatures—Gabriel said, "It's like my apartment. It looks like a complete mess, but as you look closely, you begin to see things."

True. Looking at the jumble of junk behind him, I noticed a ceramic bride and groom frozen in their happiness beside a jolly plaster pizza man in a baker's hat. Propped up against a candlestick stood a creased and dusty black-and-white snapshot of a smiling Adonis in a Speedo bathing suit—Gabriel, circa 1956—and near that, a marble-patterned school-essay notebook. Gabriel picked it up and read me his mother's last words as she died in his arms: "Son, good manners and perfect English, always." On the wall by the door hung some sort of dancing Hindu deity in jade. "It's plastic," Gabriel said, "but it works."

Most any god does, for Gabriel. "I love Zeus!" he told me one day. "He's such a wonderful god—because he's so *human*. Just the other day I asked Zeus, 'Why aren't you a god anymore?' And Zeus said, 'Gabriel, I'm not a god anymore because people stopped worshipping me.'"

Gabriel worked; he just never saved any money. He painted pictures in Andy Warhol's Factory, got a job as a diamond sorter, went into business for himself making jewelry in a garage (he accidentally burned it down), and finally got a job calculating the wages and hours of city employees, until he had a stroke and couldn't do it anymore. In these straitened circumstances, he embarked on his true career—begging.

"I am so joyous when I am on the street," Gabriel told me. "Someone saw me taking food out of a trash can and said to me, 'Don't you have any pride?' 'No, not a bit,' I said. 'Any Catholic can tell you, pride is a sin.' Another fellow said, 'I don't give money to panhandlers.' I said, 'I'm not a panhandler. I'm a beggar. A panhandler sits with his hand out. A beggar talks to people.' It's just a joy for me to beg. I give everyone a chance to affirm their humanity. The 843rd commandment in Leviticus, I think it's the 843rd, give or take—Leviticus was added to the Bible later, during the Babylonian exile—the commandment says, 'Thou shalt not stand idly by.' Most people walk by, turning their heads away as though I'm invisible. But I'm grateful that so many people are kind."

"How many people are kind?" I asked.

"Ten percent. But that's a lot of people."

Another time, when Gabriel went to put the matzo ball soup my wife had made for him into his refrigerator, I saw a note scrawled on a white paper plate on the floor—the sort of note one might find by the body of a trapped miner. "Dying is so tedious and painful," the penciled message read. "I look so strange. I caught a glimpse of myself in the mirror and was startled."

Later, Gabriel gave me a whole bagful of his art—portraits, nudes, abstracts, landscapes. "Someday I'm going to find a gallery that will take your paintings, and I hope you make a ton of money," I told him. I wanted Gabriel to make something of himself. I wanted him to amount to something.

"I've had a fantastic life," Gabriel told me, in the nursing home. "I've been around the world. Sometimes people would say to me, 'I wish I could have gone where you went, done what you did.' I'd say, 'You could have. These are choices people make. You chose to have a wife, a family, to work.' I chose not to have those things, with the comforts they bring. To me, those were not important. Work was never important to me. I decided years and years ago what was important to me was to go here and to go there, to learn this and learn that.

"I'm a wreck, but I've lived the most extraordinary life I could live—not the most extraordinary life, but the most extraordinary life that *I could live.* Everything is a trade-off."

Now Gabriel is very sick—no surprise, when you're seventy-two and have been dumpster-diving for a decade—and I've got his health-care proxy and his power of attorney, and I'm trying to beat the nursing home to his pension checks, so that he won't lose his apartment. I wish I could straighten Gabriel's life out for him, but I can't. He made his choices.

Wednesday, August 13, 2008

Gabriel's okay! I ran into him on Court Street this afternoon and we sat down on the bench outside the Tea Room. I was looking into his eyes from just inches away. His right eye is light gray, like a wolf's. His left eye is always half closed, as a result of his stroke.

"Everything is illusion," Gabriel said.

"Epicurus says this world is reality," I replied, referring to something I'd just read and would soon forget. "What we can perceive through the senses is real."

"Yes," Gabriel agreed, "but for how long?"

A good point, and I ran into it again just a few days later in Jennifer Michael Hecht's *Doubt*, where she explains that according to some Buddhists, there are no nouns, only verbs, because everything is always changing, coming into existence and passing away. So, there is no you, only the universe you-ing, just as there are no waves, just the sea waving.

Tuesday, September 2, 2008

My whole twenty years at Time Warner were tainted by the way I was treated on that last day. I gave that company my all, but now I wouldn't piss on Time Warner if its building were on fire. (It isn't. That crackling sound you hear is my bridges burning.)

Was it really necessary for them to treat me as untrustworthy and presumed dangerous on layoff day? The short answer is no, according to management consultant David Gebler, who advises global companies on business ethics, corporate culture, and what he calls "values-based decision-making." I met with him in his large but not ostentatious home in an affluent Boston suburb.

"Why do companies hustle you out the door when you're laid off these days?" I asked him.

"There is a view from the HR perspective that it's better for the survivors to not have malingerers around," he replied. "I think that's an insensitive approach—to assume that the survivors want to get these people out of the way as soon as possible so that they can get on with their work. It's completely contrary to human nature. People's reaction is 'Jim's been my friend for ten years; I want to make sure he's okay.' You should make the survivors feel good that the people leaving are being treated respectfully. To me, this should be common sense."

"Is there a right way to lay people off?" I asked.

"Yeah, there's definitely a right way to do it," Gebler said. "It's really about asking, 'How can we do this in a way that's most respectful?' Twenty-year veterans—do you have to terminate them on one day's notice, without allowing them to have access to their stuff? What's the risk if you give them two weeks' notice, or two months' notice, or keep them on as a contract worker?

"People hate being lied to, so give people honest information. Engage the workforce with what the issues are, so they perhaps can be part of the solution. Like, 'Guys, we have to save fifteen percent of our costs. Is there anything we can do to accomplish that short of layoffs?'

"Look at Malden Mills, when Aaron Feuerstein was having to lay off people," Gebler continued. "People were cheering him, because they felt that he did everything he could to save their jobs. What I cite in his case is just this level of openness. He said, 'We will keep you on as long as we can.' Then once they were going into bankruptcy, he said, 'Our business is changing. I can't sustain it anymore, and this is what's happening.' The people appreciated him being open and honest with them. They applauded him for treating them with respect."

Tuesday, October 14, 2008

Aaron Feuerstein agreed to talk to me at his summer home in the central Massachusetts town of Berlin. I followed a winding country road up a hill to a restored eighteenth-century farmhouse set on rolling lawns opposite a dairy farm. In the driveway sat a maroon 1997 Cadillac STS with vanity plates reading MALDEN.

I'd read up on Feuerstein. He was proud of Malden Mills, the textile company founded by his grandfather in 1906, proud that its employees had invented Polartec, a synthetic thermal fabric made from recycled plastic, and proudest of all that the company was still located in Lawrence, Massachusetts, long after other textile firms had abandoned New England in pursuit of cheap labor.

Feuerstein had just gotten back to his condo in Brookline from his seventieth birthday party on the night of December 11, 1995, when he got an urgent phone call. An explosion had set one factory building on fire, and the icy 40 mph winds had spread the flames to two others. He and his wife and son drove the thirty miles to Lawrence in time to see the buildings burn to the ground.

The next day, Feuerstein announced to a crowd of cheering workers that he would continue to pay all 3,100 of them while he rebuilt the factory. His commitment to his employees made Feuerstein a household name for a while. *People* magazine even did a story on him. He was invited to the White House and received twelve honorary degrees for setting such a noble example—so noble that it would never be followed, as it turned out.

I knocked on the farmhouse door. An elderly man with a senatorial shock of white hair greeted me and led me into the living room.

I told Feuerstein what I knew of his story, and asked for some particulars.

"When did you decide to keep paying people?" I asked.

"Right that night," he replied. "My recollection is that the whole mill yard was mobbed with people watching the fire and weeping over the fact that the last important employer in Lawrence was going under. So when I saw it, I only thought in terms of what

I could do to remain in business, to continue to employ these excellent Lawrence laborers and hold everything together."

The numbers involved were so hard to believe I checked to see if I had them right. "Seven months after the fire you finally had to lay off 450 people, and you gave them six months' severance. So that's thirteen months you paid them?"

"Yes," he said. "We considered the worker a stakeholder in our enterprise. We had a mission of making the best quality in the world, and I couldn't make that without the worker. The worker deserved what I did."

"I've heard that people actually applauded you when you were laying them off, because they knew you had done the best you could," I said, recalling what the management guru Gebler had told me. "Is that true?"

"It is true," said Feuerstein. "I think the reason that the workers took it in a more understanding way than people usually do when informed they are laid off was that, contrary to my advisors, I insisted I would personally go up there and make the announcement and tell them honestly what the problem was and why we were doing it."

(Malden Mills collected $300 million from insurance but was spending $450 million, much of it borrowed, to rebuild, and its creditors were growing concerned about its ability to repay.)

"Most people say the way you have to do it is on the last day of work, you inform them that they will never work again, and it's done by some manager somewhere telling them, so that they can cause the least amount of trouble in their anger," Feuerstein continued. "I decided I would do it a different way, and that if they were angry, they had every right to be angry, and they would be angry to my face, and I would just be there and take the medicine.

"I told them how much they had contributed to the company and how meaningful it was, and that I didn't consider them just a pair of hands—and I guess as a result of that, they not only took it well, but they tried their best to let me understand that they didn't hold any grudge against me, and they thanked me for all the years of employment that they had. It was an amazing thing. They actually came over one after another and embraced me.

"You know, it's interesting," he went on. "After the fire I received over ten thousand letters from people all over the country who were moved by what happened at Malden, and the overwhelming majority of them were working people. And the gist of the letters was that they extended loyalty to the corporations where they were working, and that that loyalty was never returned to them."

In the end, Malden Mills went bankrupt and Feuerstein lost control of the company, but he clearly had no regrets—nor was he boastful or self-righteous or angry. He just seemed solid, really grounded somehow.

"Your respect for working people and concern for the community—where do those values come from?" I asked.

"It grows out of the Jewish Bible, the Hebrew Bible," Feuerstein replied. "There are three statements that I consider the basis for my philosophy. One is in Genesis where it says, 'And God created man in His image.' All humans have a divine spark, and we have, as a result of it, a social responsibility, which I believe is the basis of the French demand for equality and fraternity, and it's at the core of the American Declaration of Independence—that all men are created equal. So that idea that a man has a divine spark is crucial.

"The other thing is in Leviticus 19:18, 'V'ahavta l'reiachah kamocha.' Love thy neighbor as thyself. It's a hard thing to do. But we as human beings have a social responsibility. And then, in my particular case, I was tremendously moved by Deuteronomy 24:14 and 15 where it says: 'You cannot oppress the working man because he is poor and needy. Each day you have to give him his wages.'

"So it's as clear as it can be that those who participate in the work of this world cannot be oppressed," Feuerstein concluded. "I think it's as simple as that, I really do."

Thursday, October 16, 2008

Shaving this morning, I hear some expert on Bloomberg Radio saying, "Baby boomers thought they'd be able to sell their house for twice what they bought it for and retire, and that's not going to happen. They'll be happy to work as a greeter at Wal-Mart."

So now the issue may not be finding meaningful work, but finding *any* work. Here's what I wonder: If ten million of us are out of work in this country, yet the world continues to function pretty much as it did before, what were we doing?

Tuesday, October 21, 2008

The AOL home page features a story, BEST PART-TIME GIGS FOR BABY BOOMERS. Nationwide, Wal-Mart lists 960 available part-time and full-time jobs for retail store associates, assistant managers, and store managers, and UPS has 699 openings for part-time package handlers and driver helpers.

Both companies say that they value their people above all else. At the UPS website under "What We Believe," it says: "UPS believes its people are its most valuable asset." Wal-Mart's site proclaims that the "guiding principles Sam Walton founded his company upon in 1962 are still the beliefs we follow today," and first among these is "Respect the Individual—'Our people make the difference' is not a meaningless slogan. It's a reality at Wal-Mart."

Oh my, who said anything about a meaningless slogan? Why would management at Wal-Mart assume that *anyone* would think 'Our people make the difference' was a meaningless slogan?

Who wrote that part about a "meaningless slogan"? Fire him!

Monday, November 10, 2008

Wandering through Barnes & Noble, my attention is grabbed by a book with a cover photo of a young woman's tensely knit hands resting on her lap above bare knees. That's it. The rest of her is beyond the edges of the cover. It's a trend on book covers these days—parts of women's bodies, no faces. (Often very sexy. Why?)

Anyway, the book, by Susanna Sonnenberg, is called *Her Last Death: A Memoir*, and I read on the back cover that it's a courageous true account: When a young woman in Montana learns that her mother is in a coma and near death thousands of miles away, she cannot bring herself to go to her mother's side. She resents her mom's horrific parenting: "With outrageous behavior and judgment tinged by drug use, she taught her child the art of sex and the benefits of lying," according to the cover copy. And I'm thinking, why are books always about people struggling to overcome the damage inflicted by parents who were crazy or abusive or addicted? What about the rest of us, whose parents weren't crazy or abusive? What is it that we have to overcome, or come to grips with? We live in absolute ignorance of normal life, or what normal life is supposed to be.

Leaving the store (I was just browsing), I happen across a table piled high with paperback copies of *Man's Search for Meaning* by Viktor Frankl. MORE THAN 12 MILLION COPIES IN PRINT WORLD-WIDE, it says in a circle emblazoned on the sky-blue cover, and not one of them had ever found its way to me.

Monday, November 24, 2008

"Man's search for meaning is the primary motivation in his life . . . ," writes Frankl, a psychiatrist who gained a certain perspective on what keeps people going during the two and a half years he was imprisoned in Nazi concentration camps.

"Sometimes," he notes, "the frustrated will to meaning is vicariously compensated for by a will to power, including the most primitive form of the will to power, the will to money."

If only I believed in money—a daily goal, a long-term plan, its own reward! Or things. Or the renunciation of things. Missed my chance for all that. It's hard to renounce materialism when materialism is renouncing you.

The feeling of meaninglessness "has become a universal phenomenon in our industrial societies," especially among people suffering from "unemployment neurosis," Frankl goes on. "I could show that this neurosis really originated in a twofold erroneous identification: being jobless was equated with being useless, and being useless was equated with having a meaningless life."

He had a prescription for his unemployed patients: Do volunteer work.

"[A]s soon as they could fill their abundant free time with some sort of unpaid but meaningful activity," Frankl observes, "their depression disappeared although their economic situation had not changed. . . ."

Okay, doctor's orders: I'll keep teaching English at the Arab American Association, even though half the time no one shows up.

Monday, February 2, 2009

Once, when I was that nineteen-year-old author I mentioned at the beginning, an enterprising high school senior invited me to give a talk at his school, in a Connecticut mill town. (Maybe it was Waterbury?) I don't remember what I said, but it was probably something about how the powerful pitted working people against one another, and how if everyone would get together and stop chasing after the useless crap advertising makes us want, we could all be a lot happier. Something like that.

Afterwards, my host invited me over to his home.

Just as I walked into his house, down the stairs came this blonde vision in a diaphanous nightgown. In the middle of the afternoon. His older sister. She turned on a dime and went back up to her room. And yet that is not the most memorable thing that happened.

Later, somehow, I was sitting with the sister and her father at their kitchen table. A working man, lean, with strong hands, he asked me how I liked writing for a living. "It's really hard," I said, "but it beats bolting bumpers on Chevettes."

"You're right about that," her father said. "I worked on an assembly line, and I thought about killing myself many times."

He was just agreeing with me, not slapping me across the face and denouncing my ignorance and pretension, but it hit me with great force that what was a figure of speech to me—I'd never actually bolted bumpers on Chevettes—was a painful reality to him. That was the most memorable thing that happened.

I remain keenly aware of the limits of my experience, and from time to time I make an effort to learn about other people's lives. So I phoned auto worker Ed Booth after I saw him quoted in a Newark (Delaware) *News Journal* story about Chrysler employees who continued to do their jobs after being told that their factory was closing forever:

> *Plant workers have been working overtime this week to meet Chrysler's production goals. In spite of the difficult conditions, workers have stayed focused on assembling the plant's final batch of vehicles, said Ed Booth III, a team leader on the plant's assembly line. "The work force at Newark is an exceptional work force," said Booth, a 20-year veteran of the plant. "They do the job and they do it well."*[21]

I explained to Booth that I was writing about work and the loss of work, and asked if I could come down and talk with him. He

21 "Chrysler's Stamp on Delaware History Comes to End Today; Assembly Plant Set to Ship Final Vehicles," by Andrew Eder, *News Journal*, December 19, 2008.

was initially unenthusiastic ("What's in it for me?" he inquired—a very good question), but after thinking it over for a few days he decided to give me a chance.

I found Booth's double-wide manufactured home on three-quarters of an acre of flat land surrounded by more flat land amid the woodlands and cornfields of southern Delaware. He'd bought the place a few years before, intending to retire there someday—but suddenly someday, thanks to Chrysler Corporation, had arrived early. Now, clad in a gray T-shirt that matched his close-cropped hair, Booth sat across from me at a little kitchen table surrounded by cardboard boxes packed with the contents of the home where he and his former wife had raised their three daughters. That home was a hundred miles north, near the plant where, until a month ago, Booth had installed glass on Dodge Durango SUVs.

I asked Booth to give me a quick rundown of his work history.

"I started working at the Chrysler plant in March of 1989," he recalled. "I am fifty-five now, so I was about thirty-five. The very first job I ever did there was dashboards. The dash was already in the truck; you had twenty-one screws and you hooked up the radio, the [instrument] cluster, the cigarette-lighter, everything on the dash. You did every fifth car, and at that point we were building roughly five hundred vehicles a day, so I was doing a hundred vehicles. I got home, I couldn't hardly get out of my car.

"I swore I was never going back, that first day. But I got up the next day and said, 'I feel a little better. All right, let me try it another day,' and by the end of the second week when I got the paycheck, I said, 'Well, maybe I can stick to this a little bit longer, but I am not staying forever. I am going to find another job.' And that was twenty years ago."

Before Chrysler, Booth had installed monitoring equipment in people's homes for Arbitron, the audience-ratings firm; he'd fixed copying machines ("Great job—just not enough money"); and he'd had his own electronics repair business, "working on everything from wheelchairs to tattoo needles to anything people brought me. I was an authorized Atari service center, authorized ColecoVision, authorized Intellivision. I did it all. For eight years I had a good life.

"To take it all the way back," Booth concluded, "when I graduated high school in 1971—I got married and had a kid on the way; I was seventeen—I was working at Midway Getty as head mechanic and manager of the station."

"How did you know enough to be head mechanic?" I asked.

"Doing it on my own, just picking it up, talking to people, looking in books and trying it," Booth said. "In high school I built my own cars; I built race engines. My first project, I had my engine completely apart and each piece painted and laid out to dry. My dad looked around and said, 'You will never get that back together again.' A week later it was up and running."

I could see in Booth's face that he could see in my face that I was extremely impressed.

"Tell me about work at the Chrysler plant," I said. "Can you describe a typical day?"

"You get to work a little early," he began. "I'd usually get there at 5:00 [a.m.]. You get the tools set up, get whatever you might need. Maybe the night shift left you down on supplies, so you'd have to carry them over to the table. You don't get paid till 5:30.

"At 5:30, the bell went off, and you started working, and then we had a break at 7:15 and 9:15; 11:00 was lunch. The first two breaks were fourteen or fifteen minutes, and a half-hour for lunch.

"Now, take the windshield job, for instance. The windshield would come up, you had to wipe with an alcohol wipe the front flange, the side glass flange, and half of the back glass flange. Then you would have to put the front IP [instrument panel] cover on; the guy on the other side would assist you. So you had to build that up, put it on, snap it in, lock it in; then you'd have to guide the windshield in, align it side to side, tap it down. Doing that 317 times a day, over and over again, just being on your feet is enough to kill you. It's noisy; there's no ventilation; it's almost like you can't breathe, it gets so hot."

"What about the mental aspect of the work?" I asked. "How do you maintain your concentration?"

"Once you get the hang of the job, you don't need concentration," said Booth. "After a while, in fact, there were points when I actually would do the job with my eyes closed and do everything by feel just to see if I could, just to break the monotony.

"However, if you had anything on your mind that was disgruntling you, that was destroying you, it'd just give you nothing but time to think about it. So if, say, you just went through a divorce, and your life is in turmoil, and you don't know what you are going to do, that's all you had to think about for eight to ten hours.

"Somebody asked me once, 'Can you describe what your job is like?' I said, 'Take a Chinese checkerboard, put it on a table, and take each Chinese checker and hit every hole and move it across the board, and when you get done turn it around and go back the other way, and then do that for eight hours, and that's about what it is mentally to you. Do that for eight hours, stopping every hour and forty-five minutes for fourteen minutes to go get a drink of water, go to the bathroom, and then come back and do it again. Now do that for sixty hours a week.'

"Mentally, it's very menial. You like to think you're better at it than anybody else, and you probably are, because you are doing it so much. But nowhere is it rewarding as far as, 'Look what I did.' We take pride in our work. We like the fact that we can say we built three hundred trucks, and I know every one I did is perfect. But as far as, 'I invented this today. I really used my head today,' it's not there."

"Do you think Chrysler treated its employees fairly over the years?" I asked.

"They took care of the upper management," Booth replied, "and the only thing that used to hurt me is, if upper management didn't come in, the United Auto Workers could build that truck without them. We didn't need them for anything. As long as the parts got there, we could build that vehicle. If the union workers didn't come in, they couldn't build a single unit. We would get a profit-sharing check of $300 or $400, and the supervisor would get $80,000. And we're doing all the work. So that kind of peeves you a little bit. But other than that—I mean, Chrysler's paying the bills. I got no grudges against Chrysler."

Around the time I met Booth, just about everything you heard or read said auto workers' wages, benefits, and pensions had driven GM and Chrysler into bankruptcy. I asked him about this.

"I was watching TV," he responded, "and the woman announcer on air was talking to one of the Ford or GM or Chrysler officials, and she said, 'You have over 250,000 people out there getting enormous pensions.' And I am thinking, 'Enormous pensions! If I got the full pension it would just be good enough to live on.'

"Okay, we are walking out of there with a decent pension, but we are also crippled. I have got one bad knee, one bad ankle, two ruptured discs in my lower back, two ruptured discs in my neck. I have got tennis-elbow, and I have got carpal tunnel starting in both hands. There are guys walking in with canes, walking out with canes, still working. I mean it's a tough life, it really is. People who say, 'Oh, they are making great wages and great pensions,' put them in there for one day."

I told Booth a little about my own layoff, especially the part about being presumed dangerous and barred from the building. "After Chrysler announced that the plant was going to close in ninety days," I asked him, "weren't people throwing monkey wrenches into the transmissions?"

"There was some keying of the sides of the trucks," said Booth, "and people just not giving a darn, letting things go undone and unplugged. Myself, I didn't do anything like that. I was a little upset, but I did business as usual. I guess it's work ethics. I am there to do the job; they are paying me to do a job."

u miss anything about working at Chrysler?"

eople, the other workers. That's pretty much all you miss, except for the money, of course. The other thing was, when you walked out of there at the end of the day, you didn't bring your work with you. That's one good thing about assembly-line work: When you leave, you are done. Because I have worked jobs where I take it home; that's the worst thing, because you can't sleep. Like I am sure you—when you leave—you are going to be thinking about this talk we're having all the way home: 'What am I going to do with it?'"

When we first started talking, Booth had warily kept his distance from me. Two hours later, he was inside my mind.

"If you could have any job, what would it be?" I asked, by way of wrapping up.

"Oh, probably my own business again, the electronics repair shop," Booth said wistfully. (He was forced into bankruptcy when several key manufacturers decided to service their own products and terminated their authorized-repair-shop networks.) "That was probably the best times. I enjoyed doing everything. Everything I did was for me—me and the family. If I worked real hard and made money, I made money for us; I didn't make it for the boss."

Ed Booth gave me a pretty good template for the ideal job: Work at something you enjoy and do well; make decent money; don't get exploited. A tall order.

Sunday, February 8, 2009

As I'm waiting to pay for a birthday card, I see a mug for sale bearing the words THE PAST IS HISTORY. TOMORROW IS MYSTERY. TODAY IS A GIFT. —ELEANOR ROOSEVELT.

Is it possible to take advice from a mug? Can you trust it? (Maybe not: Wisdomquotes.com attributes the quote to one

Babatunde Olatunji, not Eleanor.) Anyway, what does it me.
Live in the present? Okay. Will do.

Tuesday, February 24, 2009

Would it be a mistake to start taking a reduced pension now, at
age sixty? I made an appointment to see my accountant. In a mad
rush not to be late, I missed the bottom stair going into the subway at Borough Hall. Flew through the air in slow motion till the
concrete floor rushed up to meet my knees.

"Are you all right?" a Samaritan (one of the good ones)
asked.

"Yeah, I'm okay," I said. "No, wait . . . Fuck!! I'm not okay!
I can't move my leg."

Ambulance, hospital, broken knee cap. Welcome to never
being quite the same.

Monday, March 9, 2009:

Had knee surgery Friday and will be on crutches for some time.
This may be God's way of saying that it would be okay for me
to stop schlepping out to the Arab American Association on
Wednesday nights, as I have for the past two years. At most, one or
two men show up for my English lessons, anyway. Maybe they're
not the greatest lessons. Time to move on.

Saturday, March 14, 2009

"You can't have a fear of the unknown," the artist/beggar Gabriel
Fluke tells me, apropos of nothing. "You have a fear of the known.
You have a fear of what you know."

Well, I point out, people are afraid of death. That's a fear of
the unknown.

etty much know," Gabriel replies. "That's why
a can't fear what you don't know."

arch 18, 2009

I SAY SOMETHING ABOUT MY LEG HURTING, AND A SHRINK JOKES THAT I'M GOING TO TAKE IT OFF AND PRETEND IT'S NOT MINE ANYWAY. THE SHRINK AND I COME UP WITH A PLAN: PUT ALL MY SINS AND REGRETS IN ONE LEG AND THEN PRETEND IT'S NOT MINE.

Monday, April 6, 2009

I'm writing a freelance article about a new micro-credit lending program for low-income women in Queens. Lillie, an eighty-two-year-old black woman in a white baseball cap, told me that a small loan enabled her to help a nephew get started in an airport-van-service business, and that she herself had worked all her life as a garment presser in a dry-cleaning shop.

"That's hot work," I said, trying to show appreciation and respect.

Lillie thought I said "hard work" and replied, "All work is hard. You sit down and push a pencil and you have to figure out what to say, that's hard."

I was astonished at her kindness—putting my labor on a level with hers.

Perhaps sensing that I was open to instruction, she changed the subject. "When you're little, you say 'That's Jesus,' out there," she told me. "When you grow up, Jesus is in your mind. When you say 'I want to help that person, or I know how that person feels,' that's Jesus in you."

Lillie says God has a plan for us, but we can't know what it is.

Tuesday, May 26, 2009

I'm rewriting articles for *Waterkeeper*, the magazine of the Waterkeeper Alliance, a group of two hundred organizations worldwide that works to preserve and restore the world's waters. Waterkeepers, baykeepers, riverkeepers, coastkeepers, wetlands-keepers—they all know that without water, nothing means anything, and they fight for every drop.

I take raw copy sent in by members and turn it into stories like HOPE ON THE HALF SHELL: NY/NJ BAYKEEPERS' OYSTER RESTORATION PROJECT TURNS THE TIDE FOR NEW YORK'S LEGENDARY BIVALVE, or CHARLSTON WATERKEEPER'S FIRST CLEANUP A SUCCESS.

As I talk on the phone with these activists, I'm always impressed by their sense of mission. They leap out of bed in the morning to *save the water*. But rewriting *Waterkeeper* doesn't do that for me. Somehow the job just doesn't seem . . . I don't know . . . *wet* enough.

Wednesday, May 27, 2009

My daughter, Halley, called, as she often does, to tell me about her day. The instant I heard her voice, an epiphany—*This is my life.* I love my children; I love my wife.

Centered. Complete. For a moment I was.

Tuesday, June 2, 2009

I look out my window and see a young man with a shaved head walking down the street holding a little plastic capsule on a cord in front of his mouth, talking loudly. Right on his heels, another dude strides down the sidewalk with large gray headphones clamped over his ears, staring straight ahead.

Why do I resent these people so much? Why should I care if they choose to remain tethered to electronic devices, oblivious to the physical world around them? Birds are singing their evening songs. The spring-green trees are dripping from this afternoon's thundershower. The air is fragrant with wet grass. The cell-phone yappers are oblivious to it all, their minds engaged in conjuring a person not present, a place not here. It's their loss. What's it to me? I guess what galls me is their indifference to all I hold dear, their contempt for—how shall I say it?—*me*.

And what's really depressing is that I know it is never going to get better. It is only going to get worse. Cell phones give way to smartphones give way to voice-activated eyeglasses with touch-screen GPS navigation systems. Look on the bright side: If all these people abandon reality, there's more reality for me. *Mine, all mine!*

Monday, June 8, 2009

I apply online for a volunteer position at the International Rescue Committee, teaching refugees English at the IRC office and in their homes. Hopefully, I can worm my way into a paying job. Of course, I'll get paid a lot less for doing useful work than for the pointless but profit-oriented activity I engaged in near the tip of the corporate pyramid, where, if you skim even a little from the fruits of the labor of each person below, you make out like a bandit; but I must get paid *something*. People will say, "Here, Jim, here is some money. Now go and teach these refugees to speak; give them their voices back." Or, "Here . . . here is money for their stories that you get from them, or even your story about getting their stories. Your empathy is so excellent you enable us to feel their pain (without it actually hurting), a deeply moving experience that makes us feel alive and worthy of being alive. Here, take this money and keep on doing what you are doing. Save those people. Save us. Save yourself."

I must get paid.

Tuesday, June 16, 2009

"[A]t any time each of the moments of which life consists is dying, and that moment will never recur," Viktor Frankl writes. "And yet is not this transitoriness a reminder that challenges us to make the best possible use of each moment of our lives? It certainly is, and hence my imperative: *Live as if you were living for the second time and had acted as wrongly the first time as you are about to act now."*

I think what he's saying is that you should live as though this were your past—which it is—knowing that you *can* change the past, but only *right now.*

I want to go to work *right now* doing something meaningful. Unfortunately, as I search the employment listings, I find that I'm not qualified to do anything. Even entry-level jobs demand experience or skills that I don't have. Early intervention service coordinator for victims of child abuse, case aide for housing outreach and placement program for people with HIV/AIDS, activity specialist for homeless youth, counselor for adolescent runaways, case worker in a foster boarding home—I can't do any of it. I don't have strong project management experience, including managing multilayered projects with diverse internal and external stakeholders. I don't speak Spanish. I don't have two-plus years of relevant work experience in case management with children and families; extensive knowledge of local AIDS housing service providers and related resources; or prior experience with homelessness, mental health, and/or addictions—much less a bachelor's degree in a field related to human services.

If I am a knowledge worker, what do I know? I'm going to have to learn how to do something if I'm to have any hope of landing a job in the do-good industry.

A friend tells me that a good place to look for an idealistic job is at Idealist.org. The site features a photo of smiling twenty-five-year-olds. I'm not smiling. I'm not twenty-five. There is no place for me in this picture (except in an aptitude test with the question,

"Which person does not belong?"). It's like a fence with concertina wire on top and a big sign: OVER 25 KEEP OUT.

Undeterred, I sign up to attend a graduate degree fair sponsored by Idealist.org, to see if there might be some course of study that I could reasonably hope to master and complete in time to land a job before my dotage.

Thursday, June 18, 2009

A rainy Thursday evening. I can't recall at first where you change trains to get to Columbus Circle, where I went to work every day for my last five years at Time Warner. FORDHAM UNIVERSITY GRADUATE SCHOOL OF SOCIAL SERVICE it says on the door at 130 West 60th Street. I walk into a mobbed auditorium. It's impossible to wedge my way through the throng to see what's on offer at the sixty-one tables. I have only fifteen minutes until I need to leave for the panel on "When and What to Study." I look for ESL programs and find none. I see placards for "Multicultural Leadership," "Conflict Resolution," and "International Development," but I'm in a rush to get to the panel. I don't have time to talk to the program reps. I don't have time to get a master's. I don't have time to pass the New York Bar and learn immigration law. I don't have time.

The emcee of the panel discussion, a priest-y looking fellow from Fordham, opens the session to questions right after the panelists have introduced themselves. I think of asking about age as a factor in graduate-program admissions decisions—Do they think all that training would be better expended on someone who will use it for decades rather than a few years?—but I would be embarrassed. My fifty fellow would-be do-gooders in the audience are male, female, black, white, Asian, businesslike, and grunge, but they all have one thing in common: They're young, thirty at the outside. Even the panelists are under forty.

In answer to a question about the longevity of careers, the young woman from the Columbia School of Social Work, talking too softly and too quickly (a delivery bespeaking inexperience, I'd say) replies, "In social work, you can always change what you do in five years." Oh, sure, of course, because you have lots of five-year stints ahead of you, because you are not, let's say, sixty, or anything like that.

David Worley, the admissions director from the Iliff School of Theology in Denver adds, "The top ten careers of 2019 have not been invented, so think about what's timeless, what's still going to be relevant when you're sixty-five." *Timeless?* I'm going to be sixty-five in about ten minutes. I feel a twinge of nausea.

"Your future should be what you want it to be," adds the fellow from the Heller School for Social Policy and Management at Brandeis. "It should not be driven by what you've done in the past. What we do look for is what you have *gained and learned* from what you have done."

What have I learned? I have learned that, upon close examination, complicated things are simple and simple things are complicated, that every solution causes a problem, that 90 percent of overcooking is due to fear of undercooking, and that my ability to make anything happen is extremely limited at best.

A young woman asks about whether recommendations from professors are really necessary or feasible when you've been out of school for a while.

An admissions officer reassures her. "We all understand that it's better to get a letter from a nonacademic source who really knows you than to get one from a professor whose class you took nine years ago, who just pulls the transcript."

Nine years ago! He says that as though nine years were an extremely long time. What if your professors knew you *thirty-nine years* ago? What if your professors are dead? As I was rummaging around in my memory to see if I could recall the names of any of my college professors, I was yanked back to the present by the Denver divinity school guy, who was suggesting that work is actually the wrong place to look for meaning in life.

"I'm not convinced meaning isn't separate from a job or career," David Worley volunteered, out of the blue. "A lot of people come back to our institution looking for meaning. Some of them find it; some of them don't. Finding it may have more to do with the person than the job. I know that for me, personally, how meaningful what I do in a day is depends more on the state of my centered, spiritual practice than on the job itself."

What? This is exactly the opposite of what Viktor Frankl, who *wrote the book* on meaning, said: "Meaning is to be discovered in the world, rather than within man or his own psyche." So, which is it?

Somehow, as career discussions so often do, this one winds up with a discussion of law school. The young Indian woman representing the University of Southern California suggests that we consider MPA and MPP programs as alternatives to the law. These fields are growing fast, she says, and a lot of jobs that used to go to lawyers and economists now go to people with these degrees. (I'm guessing these letters stand for master's of public administration and master's of public policy—two fields that I don't think existed when I was in college; or maybe I missed the memo.) She suggests we visit PublicServiceCareers.org to learn more.

I feel like I'm too old to embark on a course of study now, but I'm reminded of an anecdote that I read years ago. It was in *Reader's Digest* or maybe *The Saturday Evening Post*, some sunny, upbeat, mainstream publication, but I took it seriously nonetheless: A man would like to go to medical school, but he says by the time he finishes in four years, he'll be fifty years old. And his friend says, "How old will you be in four years if you *don't* go to medical school?"

So, I take a look at PublicServiceCareers.org, which touts careers in "the new public sector," a complex network of governments, nonprofits, NGOs, the private sector, and universities that has emerged over the past thirty years, while I was busy with other things.

> *What makes a professional career in public service so unique is the emphasis on tackling "wicked problems"—the challenging issues that define the public agenda and call for talented individuals to devote their efforts to finding solutions. Here are just a few of the "wicked problems" on the agenda today:*
> - *Managing global climate change and controlling its underlying causes, such as carbon emissions;*
> - *supplying food, energy, and clean water to the growing populations in developing countries;*
> - *securing the United States and other countries against the possibility of chemical, biological, and nuclear terrorism;*
> - *redeveloping older urban areas that have lost their economic base in manufacturing;*
> - *transitioning recently incarcerated persons into productive, nonviolent lives in society;*
> - *ending the epidemic of HIV infection in developed and developing countries; and*
> - *providing quality education and health care to children living in poverty.*

Jeez, where to begin?

Saturday, June 20, 2009

Saw in the paper that the famous sci-fi writer Ray Bradbury offers one piece of career advice for all comers: "Do what you love. Love what you do."[22]

---

22 "At 88, A Writer Fights for Libraries, and Tells a Few of Life's Tales," by Jennifer Steinhauer, *New York Times*, June 20, 2009.

It worked for him, but can he really take his own experience and extrapolate it into a general principle? Everybody loves doing something—I love reading at the beach—but not everybody loves doing something *that you can get paid for.* And "love what you do"? What's that mean? If you can't be with the job you love, love the job you're with? Easy to say, but who loves data entry? Are data inputters supposed to love what they do?

Well, yeah, I guess, if *love* means treat the work with respect and do it the best you can. "Any job worth doing is worth doing well," my father used to say. (He didn't say anything about jobs that aren't worth doing.) I know people who do exceedingly tedious work with such grace and enthusiasm that they cheer up everyone around them: Mr. and Mrs. Oh, who operate the dry-cleaning shop on my block, and Mr. and Mrs. Yi, who run the neighborhood convenience store, and Sydrick Cardogan, who stands guard at the Time & Life Building. One thing they have in common: They're all immigrants.

Monday, June 22, 2009

"Mr. Jim!" Sydrick called out, as he emerged from the Time & Life Building on 51st Street, wearing a gray policeman's cap and a crisp shirt spectacularly white against his dark skin. We walked across the street to the Europa Cafe, one of the midtown feeding stations that receive truckloads of prepared food from New Jersey each morning and distribute it to keep the workforce humming all day. I'd explained that I was writing about work and wanted to know how Sydrick was able to maintain his friendly demeanor and positive outlook even though he's on his feet for eight hours dealing with people who slide past him day after day, year after year, without ever saying hello.

"A lot of Americans, maybe we're spoiled," I said, as we sat with our iced teas. "We're confused. We're not sure what we *want*, what we should *do*." I spoke in a whiny voice, gently mocking people like me. "Maybe immigrants like you have a better—"

"Yes," Sydrick interjected. "America's a very good country. People that come here and say they're not getting jobs . . ." He shook his head dismissively. "Most people want their field of work. But if you can't get your field of work, you got to do something else for a living. The people from the West Indies, we're really going to do what is there for us to do. You see, most of us came to this country for a living, to make life better than where we came from. Some of us did well, some didn't do well. Those that done well focus. You must focus. If you cannot focus, you cannot make life. You have to focus on something."

"And your focus has been . . . ?"

"Saving money. I started going to school for auto mechanics two or three times—I'm a mechanic; I know how to fix cars—and I had to drop out, because my wife and children needed to come up. In those days you had to show a bank statement if you were going to bring up your family. You had to show $13,000 or more. So I have to cut out all this school, and I did all the overtime, worked two jobs. At one time I was working three jobs, all in security. The first one was from 7:00 to 4:00, and the next from 5:00 to 1:00 in the morning, and then I had a good friend who would come early, so I could get relieved and get to a job at 12:00 midnight. I got a nervous breakdown. My hands used to be shaking like crazy. So I had to go from three jobs to two, and then the doctor said you have to stay with one job. So that's what I did."

"That must have been hard," I said, belaboring the obvious.

"*Real* hard," Sydrick said, "real hard. Then my wife came. She's a nurse's aide. We bought a small house, a two-bedroom house. Now we're in a three-bedroom, so I can bring up my daughters, and let them get settled down, and then work two or three more years, and then I'm going home [to Guyana]."

Sydrick is working hard at a grueling job to grab a toehold in America so that his children can be educated and succeed and make money and become lost souls like me, and it's working out. He knows what he's doing, and he knows why he's doing it.

He said you must focus on something. I've been thinking: I coached Soviet émigrés for their citizenship tests back in 2002. I tutored at the Arab American Association for two years. I've applied to volunteer at the International Rescue Committee. Reverse-engineering my life, I can see that since I've repeatedly chosen to teach immigrants, I must like it.

I'll focus on working with immigrants.

Tuesday, June 30, 2009

My wife calls this the first day of the rest of my life.

I took the 4 train to Grand Central to interview for that volunteer ESL teaching position at the International Rescue Committee. On the way, I memorized my available dates over the next few weeks, in case I was asked, so that I wouldn't have to take out my little red 2009 Standard Diary Daily Reminder book (and how long will they keep printing those, I wonder?). "What is *that?*" I imagined the young interviewer exclaiming.

Which reminds me of an aspiring captain of the universe who worked in human resources at Time Warner. When he looked askance at my date book and told me all the reasons I should switch to a PalmPilot ("You can upload your appointments to your computer!"), I replied that I had no interest in doing so, because I had Standard Diaries lined up on my bookshelf dating back to 1977 and could look up what I was doing on any day for the past thirty years. "We can always find an excuse," he sneered, with tech-ier than thou condescension. Fuck him. He lost his job before I did.

At the IRC I met Kirsten, who was in charge of education programs, and Alexis, a volunteer coordinator, both recently minted graduates of the International Education Program at Teachers College, Columbia University (another degree program that I never heard of when I was in school). They both looked about twenty-five years old, but I can't tell anymore. I was trying to listen to what Kirsten was saying while I was thinking about where to point my eyes, which, for lack of a better idea, I kept locked on hers for the whole twenty-minute interview. She asked me if I'd had any experience with immigrants. I had told her on the phone and three times in e-mails that I'd tutored immigrants at the Arab American Association for two years. I told her again. *Please*, Miss Twenty-Five-Year-Old, please allow me to work for no money.

Monday, July 13, 2009

I'm teaching English at the IRC every Monday afternoon.

I have good news for Grisha from Montenegro, Rexhap from Kosovo, Natasha from Uzbekistan, and Tsiring from Tibet—the four refugees who show up today: Although there are 171,476 words in the *Oxford English Dictionary*, the average native speaker uses only 1,200 to 2,000 in everyday speech. And half the residents of New York City don't speak English at home.

Monday, July 27, 2009

When my son, Johnny, tells me he hasn't done a couple of creative writing assignments because they were "stupid, boring bullshit," I respond angrily, sounding very much like the stereotypical father I seldom imagine myself to be: "A whole lot of life is about doing stupid, boring bullshit, and the sooner you realize that, the better off you'll be!" This is true.

Wednesday, July 29, 2009

THERE WAS A HIGH SCHOOL FOOTBALL GAME, AND THE STU-DENTS IN THE STANDS WERE ALIENATED, SILENT, STILL. ONE WAS CRITICIZED FOR TAKING A PICTURE OF A FLOWER. NOW HE WAS GOING TO TAKE A PICTURE OF HIS EAR, BUT I SAID, "DON'T. THEY DON'T LIKE INTROSPECTION.

Tuesday, August 25, 2009

I came across Esther Keeney's name while reading postings on the website of Speaking of Faith, Krista Tippett's public radio show about the Big Questions. Listeners had been invited to write in about how they'd changed their lives since the recession began.

"I quit my position as a county health nurse," Keeney wrote. "I went from a fairly lucrative income to no income at all. The [new] position (parish nurse) was made known to me the day I planned to take my life by drowning in Lake Ontario."

Whoa! That got my attention.

"I've been an RN for twelve years," the post went on. "The only way I saw to make a difference in people's lives was to get as close to the top rung of the ladder as possible (you know, to develop policies and have the power to make things happen). I reached the top as director of nursing and found out it wasn't good enough.

"The Lord gave me an avenue that fulfills all of His needs for the people in my little community. It is an incredible experience to help when you know there is no money in it. . . . I'm grateful to be alive, renewed, restored, and given a purpose in this world."

Now *there* is someone committed to having meaningful work, I thought. I found Esther Keeney in the phone book, and we agreed to meet in the Methodist church near her home in Pulaski, New York, a small, fading mill town about an hour's drive north of Syracuse.

I walked into the church's community room and encountered a tall, light-haired woman in a simple black cotton dress with colorful flowers embroidered at the collar. There was something fragile-looking about her very pale face, and as she smiled hello her blue eyes fixed on mine with an unsettling intensity.

We sat down to talk in her little office, which barely accommodated a table and two folding chairs. As we spoke, it became apparent that Keeney was fundamentally religious, but not in a fundamentalist way. She didn't quote the Bible, didn't proselytize, and didn't seem to feel she was any more right with God than I was. One more thing: When Keeney smiles—which she does often—she becomes radiant. Her eyes brighten, and light practically shines from her. Seriously. I'm not kidding.

"I wasn't getting anywhere trying to make things the way I thought they should be," she said, recounting her experience directing staff at a home-health-care agency. "You can teach the nurses and home health aides what to do, but you can't teach them the feeling they should have behind it. It's supposed to be a caring thing. The goal I had was to get people to do this because they liked to do it, and it wasn't working."

She quit and took a job with the Oswego County health department, working with patients in their homes. That didn't work out, either. "If the patient had a Bible on the table," Keeney recalled, "I would ask them what did they read today, and was it helpful, and do you have a favorite verse, and maybe say a little prayer with them or something. But no, no, no. The [nursing administrators] would call and say, 'What are you doing there so long?' They saw it as a waste."

She quit the job with the county, and couldn't think of what to do next.

Then in February 2009, her pastor approached her with a suggestion. "He said to me, 'If you want to look for something in the medical field that isn't what you've been doing, look up UMVIM, the United Methodist Volunteers in Mission,'" she recounted. "So I said, 'Yeah, okay, whatever.'

"I was depressed and didn't know it. Isn't that bad? I'm a *medical* person," she said with a chuckle. "And then on March fifteenth, it was a Sunday, I was sitting in church and I was thinking, 'What can I do in my life, because right now I haven't found anything.' I figured, 'Okay, well, nothing here. I guess I'll go home.'"

Keeney said *go home* as though she meant "go back to my house," but that's not what she meant at all.

She continued, "That's exactly what I said in my head: 'Time to go home.' It's just something takes over your whole thought process and you're not rational anymore. I knew on one side of the rock formations at Selkirk Shores [State Park] there's always deep, clear, dark water. It's beautiful. So I figured, 'Okay, I'll go there.' I know, it sounds really crazy now." She laughed at how bizarre the whole thing seemed from the vantage point of now, a completely different place.

"But after we got home from church, my husband and daughter said, 'We're going to go to Lake Ontario and take pictures of the ice formations.' I was devastated, because I was just about to leave, and I knew they were going the same place I was going." She laughed again. Coincidences, even fateful ones, seem funny in a way—the sheer unlikelihood of them. What are the odds? "And they said, 'So you want to come?'

"I said, 'No, I better get my résumé in order.' And when they left, I don't know where I went, because I was *gone*. Then I woke up—I wasn't asleep—but I woke up, and an hour had gone by. And I looked at the computer screen and the résumé program was up there, and it was completed.

"So, anyway," she said, taking a deep breath and letting it out slowly before resuming a brisk, businesslike manner of speech, "something in the back of my head said, 'Look at UMVIM,' so I clicked on the UMVIM site, and I saw this little blurb on parish nursing. The class I needed to take to become a parish nurse was in Binghamton. I drove 260 miles a day for five days to take it."

"What's a parish nurse?" I asked.

"A faith-based community nurse," Keeney replied. "We can pray with people; we can read from the Bible with them. They feel like they're not alone. It's a connection."

"Who pays you?"

"No one. It's a volunteer position. I had to start working last week again for the licensed agency—twenty hours a week—to earn money to pay for gas, because I drive around to people's homes. It's a fifty-mile radius, at least, that I'm covering."

"That's very generous of you," I observed.

"No it's not," said Keeney. "It's a directive."

"A directive from God?"

"Oh, yeah," she said matter-of-factly. "I had no idea parish nursing existed, until March fifteenth. The information was given to me three weeks before March fifteenth, but I just didn't see or hear. So, 'Guess what? You're going to hear it this time.'"

By this point I had the feeling that Keeney knew some things that I would like to learn.

"I teach English to refugees at the International Rescue Committee, in this little room with six or seven people," I confided, "and I'm enjoying it, when I'm doing it. But then I walk out into the streets of New York, and I feel like, 'This is so small. There are people arguing in court to protect the rights of *all* immigrants,' and I feel discouraged. How do you deal with the smallness of what you're doing?"

"Yeah, at first it did seem like, 'What does this little thing have to do with anything really real?'" she replied. "But the more I learn from other people, when I go into their homes and they tell me their stories, the more I see that it's a connection, and the connection doesn't end.

"This is just a little tiny connection that I'm going to tell you about: There's a lady I see once a month. She's elderly and she doesn't get around very well. She's a social person, a well-spoken, educated woman who needs people. So I was going out to see her, take her blood pressure, pray with her, go over her doctors' appointments, and I realized she needs something. She's now on our health-care team; she has a list of three people she calls once a week, and then she reports to me if there's a concern. So she's connecting with other people. They all love this phone-call thing, but they want to actually visit. So we're starting a care team that's going to visit people who are lonely. And we have a lady who makes bread—she calls it friendship bread, and she gives it to me to give to these people. These are little connections made, and it's getting wider and wider. It doesn't matter how little I do. It's what happens after me."

"And the money?" I asked. "Being paid well made me feel valued. I got a bounce in my step on payday."

"And that sense of respect from other people," she agreed. "But that sense of respect is pretty shallow, and it doesn't last very long. If you're not connecting with anybody, it all stops with you, so what's the point?"

"I understand," I said, "but you need money to keep your family safe, don't you?"

"My husband has a job," Keeney replied. "And just because you don't have the ability to go out and buy whatever is out there, that doesn't mean you're not safe. I guess it goes back to the Bible and the lilies of the field and how they don't clothe themselves and they're taken care of. I don't have any fear."

"You have faith that things will be all right?"

"Basically. That's basically my life right now: faith, and keep going. I wish I could have seen the path in front of me without going through the worst hour of my life," Keeney concluded. "You don't have to be on the brink of diving into Lake Ontario in order to see it. That's how it happened to me, because I'm sort of stubborn and didn't listen three weeks beforehand.

"But I've learned to listen, not just to my conscience or God's words coming in, but listen to other people, too. In fact, most of the time that's where the focus is, listening to other people. I never saw the important things that connect people. I always thought it was doing more, doing the most you can, instead of seeing where the most important things are. Now, I don't know, you just see it differently. *Everything is different now.*"

Esther Keeney made a big impression on me. Lessons:

1. Feeling valued because you're paid well doesn't take you very far.

2. It's *really* important to have work you find meaningful.

3. Small-bore isn't small if you're making connections with people.

Thursday, August 27, 2009

An editorial in the *Boston Globe*, EDWARD KENNEDY, 1932–2009, says that when Robert F. Kennedy was killed in Los Angeles in June 1968, Teddy understood that he would have to realize the ambitions of his brothers and parents. Unlike "most people," he would not get to choose his own path, the editorialist observes. "Most people spend their careers trying to match their skills to endeavors that are meaningful and rewarding for them."

Actually, *most people* don't have careers, and they spend their working lives trying to make ends meet any way they can—and that's in developed countries. In the rest of the world, billions of people spend their lives struggling just to stay alive.

That editorial was written by a privileged person. Trust me; it takes one to know one.

Wednesday, September 16, 2009

Being unemployed, I can finally find time to do things like read the century-old diary of my great-uncle Julius, an immigrant from Austria-Hungary.

When I open the little tan notebook, my fingers touch the leather that his fingers touched, and I can see his hand's motion in the writing. NAGASAKI, JAPAN, 1908, it says inside the front cover at the top, and at the bottom, REV. 196256, RIFLE 32589. Julius was in the US Army Signal Corps. The diary recounts (in English, his second language) his journey from his home in Boston out to California and across the Pacific and back; his admission to the Presidio Hospital in San Francisco in June 1908 with a tumor in his right leg; the amputation of his leg; the routine generosity of friends ("Sgt. Stoneman invites me to come and live with him for the winter"); and, starting in 1909, his persistent efforts to become an educated American.

Jan. 14, 1909:

Have decided to live with my friend Stoneman for a month at least. I am to board with a soldier family who live next door. By the way I would like to say that I am very well aware that my grammar as well as my mode of construction and also my way of expressing ideas are terribly at fault, but as however this is not written for publication I do not feel criminaly responsible. So if you read this you have yourself to blame.

Jan. 21, 1909:

Have been studying grammar the past few days and have just discovered that I am up against it; but maybe that when I get my great brain in working order it will not be so difficult to remember rules and not so easy to forget them after having once learned them.

Jan. 23, 1909:

I am still pounding away at that Grammar and Sgt. Stoneman makes me recite; sometimes I think I shall never learn certain things but at other times I feel quite encouraged to continue. Have sent a letter to sister Reasa asking her to give me a list of subjects studied in the eighth grade in schools of Boston and to give me names of books used so that I may work on them.

Feb. 2, 1909:

I have sent a letter of inquiry to the "Board of Simplified Spelling," which has its offices in New York, as I may be able to help them a mite; above all I do believe that there is lots of room for improvement in the spelling of English and I am anxious to see them start the ball arolling.[23]

Sept. 15, 1909:

My school days have commenced. I am taking a special course at the Boston YMCA, the subjects are Algebra, Geometry, Physics, Chemistry, Mechanical Drawing and Electricity.

April 22, 1910:

Now the question of what I am to do stares me in the face. As I shall not be able to wear an artificial limb for several

---

23 Julius is referring to Andrew Carnegie's campaign to simplify English spelling by making sensible changes such as "through" to "thru" and "though" to "tho."

months, at least, if ever. And there is too much walking and car riding and crowd jamming and stair climbing for me, with crutches I am forced to give up any idea of continuing my attendance at school. But knowing that for financial reasons I shall be unable to continue school next year [anyway]. This does not strike me as hard as it otherwise would. There are three fields open for me strictly speaking; they are one and the same thing that is, telegraphing for a railroad, commercial telegraph company, or a wireless company.

Julius makes his way to New York City, hoping that as an army-trained telegrapher he can find work—not "meaningful" work, *any* work. He spends day after day waiting around in the offices of the Marconi Wireless Co., the Lackawanna Railroad, Staten Island Rapid Transit, and Western Union, and gets nothing. In some cases he suspects he's not hired because he's missing a leg. In others, he's explicitly told so.

July 5, 1910:

Have been to see the Chief Dispatcher of the Susquehanna R.R. in Jersey City he wanted to give me a position but the officials above him decided against employing a man minus a limb.

Finally, he gets a break.

July 6, 1910:

The Postal Telegraph Co. offered me a job at Greenwich, Conn. and I accepted. Altho the pay is but $40[24] per month.

---

24 $900 in 2011 dollars.

Still I consider myself fortunate to get the opportunity of getting my hand in.

July 7, 1910:

Went to work. Found a furnished room with very nice people. My hours are from 12 to 1 Pm. 3 to 6 and 7 to 11 Pm. thus giving me all Am. to myself.

The whole morning to himself. What more could a person want? Julius asked for very little. All he wanted out of life was life itself.

March 24, 1912:

Have bought a set of the "Harvard Classics." Expect to spend many an enjoyable hour reading them. This is the first thing I ever bought on the installment plan.

April 16, 1912:

I am experiencing a steady more or less painful "stitch" on the right side between the hip and lower ribs.

April 18, 1912:

The pain in the side and back was quite severe last night.

A friend thinks the liver may be involved and recommends to Julius that he take calomel and soda.[25]

---

25 Calomel, also called mercurous chloride, was commonly used as a purgative at the time.

April 19, 1912:

Took the Calomel & Soda. The pain in the side is very much reduced, in fact it is quite gone. And think I ought to get rid of it if I reach the particular spot in that "liver" of mine with the proper dope.

Here the diary ends.

Tuesday, October 6, 2009

As long as I'm teaching ESL, I might as well learn to do it right; and if I'm ever going to get paid for it, I'll need some kind of certification, so I'm looking for a place to take a course. Went to a presentation by TESOL Training International in an old garment-district office building on Broadway, near 31st Street.

The city has two kinds of office buildings: corporate head-quarters, with their vast lobbies and big, fast elevators, and these anonymous, soot-stained relics, with little foyers and cramped, slow elevators. As I watched the tiny elevator's door slide shut a few inches in front of my face, the full weight of low-money, low-status life settled on my shoulders, making me profoundly weary. I call this Small Elevator Syndrome.

The young Indian man making a presentation on what TESOL Training International had to offer was difficult to understand. He spoke sketchy English with a heavy accent, saying, at one point, that ESL students will want us to "learn them the TOEFL test."[26] He focused on how the training would enable us to instantly land jobs just about anywhere in the world, although he did note that "in Dubai they want older people—twenty-seven,

---

26 The Educational Testing Service's Test of English as a Foreign Language.

twenty-eight years old." He seemed unnervingly eager to close the deal; you'd get a big discount if you signed up before leaving the room. I felt as though I'd stumbled into an infomercial and didn't buy it.

Tuesday, October 20, 2009

In addition to teaching a class at the IRC office, I've been assigned to tutor an Iraqi refugee family. Alexis from the IRC introduced me to them today at their home, a neat, two-story row house in the until recently Italian American, now globally diverse Brooklyn neighborhood of Bay Ridge.

The father of the family, Muhie, a salt-and-pepper-haired man in a tweed jacket and striped tie, and his wife, Suad, wearing a gray head scarf, welcomed us into the living room, where the TV was tuned to CNN at full volume. Their son Tholfikar, who resembled the actor Elliott Gould, stood off to the side while the rest of us got acquainted.

Muhie said in somewhat halting English that he had a doctorate in chemistry from a French university, was fluent in French, and had taught at the university in Baghdad. "There I am professor, but here I am . . ." He shrugged his shoulders.

"You're starting again," I said.

Muhie volunteered that he and his wife do not like politics and never have, but to teach in the university, you had to join Saddam's party. When the regime changed, he and his family had to get out of Iraq—exactly why, he didn't say.

Suad, who spoke almost no English, looked at me and nodded to show that she was listening but not understanding.

We agreed that I would come once a week for two and a half hours to tutor Muhie and Suad in English.

Friday, October 23, 2009

Worked with Muhie and Suad at their dinner table. We spent forty-five minutes going over one supermarket circular. You don't realize how complicated things are until you try to teach them. Turns out that grocery ads utilize a dizzying array of pricing schemes: "Potatoes 10 lb. bag $1.99," but "Apples, avg. bag 3 to 5 lbs., $2.99 a pound," not $2.99 a bag. There are prices per cont. (container), pkg., bag, carton. Some "conts." are "2 for $6." Does that mean one for $3? I still don't know. I think it varies.

What I learned today: The Arabic words for *tea, sugar,* and *carton* are basically the same as the English.

I mentioned that the numerals we use were invented in Arabia two thousand years ago. Give credit where credit is due.

Saturday, October 31, 2009

I took a job writing obits for Newsweek for very little money. A twenty-year-old started lecturing me on how hard it is to describe a scene. She said, "You can't say, 'He was only a judge.' You say, 'He was a judge only.'"

I said, "What the fuck are you talking about?" I told her I'd been at Time magazine for thirty-five years.

At Newsweek, I had real problems. I had just a cubicle; everyone was talking; it was cold, and the lights went out; elevators stopped. People were sabotaging things because they were being laid off.

Monday, November 2, 2009
English Class at the International Rescue Committee
Today: Prepositions

In class:
    Natasha, Ukraine, Staten Island
    Kunchok, Tibet, Queens
    Miriam, Sudan, Bronx
    Abrahim and his wife Zouyoudi, Chad, Queens
    Tsiring (a new, different Tsiring), Tibet, Queens
    Grisha, Montenegro, Queens

With the New York City Marathon so much in the air, I brought up the difference between "in" as it relates to *duration* and "in" as it relates to *when*, as in: "I will run the marathon in two hours (it starts in two hours)" versus "I will run the marathon in two hours (it will take me two hours to run it)."

Natasha asked, "Why can't we say, 'I will run the marathon *for* two hours'?"

I thought about that for a minute and figured out that "for" means how long you will do something, and "in" means how short (quickly) you will do something.

It's easy to see why I don't speak any other languages; they're hard.

As Natasha pressed me for further explanation, I realized that "in" not only means how quickly, but also means *to completion*, whereas "for" denotes how long, and *not necessarily to completion*. I will read this newspaper "in two hours" means the whole thing, that fast;[27] "for two hours" means *and then I'll stop*, whether I'm done or not. I pointed out that no American on the street knows any of this, and they shouldn't worry about it.

Kunchok hadn't been in for weeks. I was glad to see him so I could finally give him the New York City College of Technology catalog pages I'd copied on alarm, cable TV, and photovoltaic installation courses he could take for $700 as a feasible alternative

---

27 Of course, "in two hours" could also mean "two hours from now."

to the $13,000 course required to become the electrician he'd been in Tibet. For now, he's selling scarves, gloves, and hats in Central Park. His boss yells at him when he doesn't understand English, but Kunchok's learning a little more every day. He proudly recited some of the words he's mastered: "High quality, good price."

Tuesday, November 3, 2009

Based on my online research, I concluded that the least-scammy-sounding course for some kind of certification in ESL teaching was the CELTA program offered by an outfit called Teaching House, at St. John's University in Manhattan. (CELTA is the Certificate in English Language Teaching to Adults awarded by the University of Cambridge in England through three hundred licensed centers around the world.) This 160-hour program cost twice as much as any other ESL-training course in New York City, and I always remember what my friend John Short used to say: You'd have to be insane to charge more for something if it wasn't better.

Can anyone just sign up, pay the money, and get the certificate? Who knows? They required me to complete a lengthy and fairly challenging English grammar test, and I had to come in and go over every one of my answers with a young woman who insisted that I was wrong on some of them. She maintained that what I'd learned as the past perfect (I have eaten) is really the present perfect, and that what I know as the pluperfect (I had eaten) is called the past perfect. Times change; so do the names of tenses, I guess.

I jumped through those hoops, and today was my first day of CELTA training.

Classroom management: On the first day of class, you should put your Ss' (I've already learned to write "Ss" for "students") names on the board, smile, nod, and be positive. (This conflicts with my public school principal mother-in-law's advice: "Don't smile until Thanksgiving," but that was for kids.)

How to give instructions: Use simple language; give instructions one step at a time. If you say, "And now I thought it would be a good idea for us to do an exercise on prepositions," the students may think you're asking them to do "would be a good," whatever that means. "Open your book to page 30" is the sort of thing you want to say.

By the end of the morning I learned that I've been doing everything wrong. I don't demonstrate what I want the students to do; I don't ask ICQs (instruction-checking questions) to make sure they understand; I pass around handouts while I'm still giving instructions (students look at them and stop listening); I keep the students seated; I don't walk around and monitor them as they work; I don't have them work in pairs; I don't elicit choral responses to let everyone speak in the safety of a crowd; I make the class teacher-centric instead of student-centric by talking too much.

Later my team of four trainees met a few of the adult English-language learners we'll be practicing with. We were all instructed to introduce ourselves to one another, adding an alliterative food to our names: My name is Maya and I like mangoes. My name is Tim and I like toast. My name is Julie and I like juice. My name is Tazuko and I like tomatoes. My name is Takako and I like tacos. My name is Rinka and I like rice. My name is Yukiko and I like yams. Neat technique: Everyone, including me, remembered all the names.

Wednesday, November 4, 2009

A lesson on the simple present tense is a revelation. We use it for everything *but* the present:

1. Permanent facts: I live in New York.

2. Preferences: I like fish.

3. Daily routines: I get up at 7:00.

4.   Universal facts: Water runs downhill.

5.   The future: The movie starts at 8:00.

After swimming, I walk through the UBS Building from Seventh to Sixth Avenue on the chance that I may run into something edifying—an art or photo exhibit, perhaps. Sure enough, I encounter a big blowup of a picture taken by a NASA probe on the surface of Mars. The landscape is a boulder-strewn red desert, absolutely dry and barren. Nothing *means* anything there.

Thursday, November 5, 2009

My third day in the program, I taught my first lesson. I drew on the board six circles with one superlative at the bottom of each (oldest, friendliest, etc.), then wrote a list of six names, instructing the students to guess which name went with which superlative by asking me questions. Is Muriel the friendliest person you know? No. Is Muriel the oldest person you know? Yes. (I wrote Muriel in the circle marked *oldest*.) Then it was their turn to pair off and play the game with each other.

In feedback, the CELTA teacher Jennifer said my instructions were too long and repetitive; I should have drawn the circles on the board sooner; I should have told the students about "-est words," not "superlatives" (they don't need the grammar term); and I did too much TT (Teacher Talk). And here I'd thought I'd done well.

I'm thirty years older than all the other CELTA students (except Ed from the Bronx, who looks to be in his early fifties). They don't look like babies to me—I see them as peers—but I wonder what I look like to them. My stomach sank when a teacher called me "Ed" once, a mix-up obviously attributable to the fact that

Ed and Jim are the two old guys. But I've decided to ignore my age and just act like me, which is to say, act as though I'm thirty, and avoid mirrors as much as possible.

Saturday, November 7, 2009

I asked Muhie who forced his family to leave Iraq.

"You don't know exactly who," he replied. "It's all politics. I returned to our home from the country one day, and the windows were broken, and there were men in the streets with guns, [saying] 'You go or we kill you.'"

Were they Sunnis, and the armed men Shiites, or vice versa?

Suad replied that her mother (who had ten children, and at ninety-two is "strong like Clay, like Muhammad Ali," Muhie interjected) was mixed Shiite and Sunni. Everyone is mixed.

"The segregation is artificial," Muhie explained. "It's politics."

"I am good Muslim," Suad went on, in English. "He," she pointed at Muhie, "and Suhaib, Tholfikar, Ayass, Ali, Farah [their children], bad Muslim. I pray." She pantomimed the two hands moving up and down of Muslims at prayer or basketball fans paying homage to a star.

"Do you go to the mosque?" I asked, knowing that *mosque* was not the Arabic word for a place of worship, but unable to recall the word *masjid*, even though it's one of the five Arabic words I know (along with *zaytoun*—olive, *inshallah*—God willing, *carton*—carton, and *card*—card). "Don't go *masjid*," she replied. "Pray home." She's the only one in the family who does even that. "Don't like extremists," she said, frowning and shaking her head.

"Are there Jewish extremists in New York?" Muhie asked.

"Yes, there are Jewish extremists in New York," I said, thinking this merely a point of curiosity, not realizing until later that to Muhie and his family, it might mean they should fear for their lives. "And there are Muslim extremists and there are Christian extremists." I should have emphasized that there were very few of any of these. I will make a point to say so next time.

As I was getting my stuff together to leave, Suad walked over to the window. "The sun today," she said, which was very gratifying, as we'd done weather words last week. Then she said something in Arabic.

"She says, 'You are like family,'" Muhie told me.

Tuesday, November 10, 2009

My group has drawn as our principal instructor Lizzy, a thirty-something British life-force. Antic and animated—constantly in motion, prancing around the room, waving her arms, clapping—she conveys the most effective of all pedagogical messages: "This is fun."

In the warm-up to an exercise, always lead into the *topic* you'll be reading or talking about, not the grammar. "It's more interesting," she says, "and avoids the learners' reacting, 'Oh God, boring,' or 'I know this,' and it provides context. Without context, language means nothing."

We do an exercise that involves talking to one another about interesting jobs we have had. Angelo sold ice cream. Maya was the assistant to the editor of a Spanish-language newspaper in Boston after college; Sean was a bouncer; Magda worked at a summer camp for eight hundred rich kids; Julie is a preschool teacher for troubled children; and Tom worked at an employment agency. I was a criminal defense attorney.

They can still fit their résumés on one page, and, more important, they can write down dates without killing their chance for getting hired. My jobs date back to the middle of the last century. I graduated from high school twenty years after the end of World War II. These guys graduated from high school thirty years after the end of the Vietnam War.

I spoke today with the subject of my required Focus on the Learner paper, Bayram Karaca, who is having trouble connecting English words to the world. (I noticed that when his class was asked, "Where are your teeth?" most of the students tapped their teeth with a pencil. Bayram just wrote down the word *teeth*.)

A Kurd, Bayram lived in Istanbul, where he owned an electronics store. The Kurds are "pressed" (oppressed) in Turkey, he says. He wrote a book promoting Kurdish rights, and before it could go to "push" (press), the government looked at it and he got in trouble. His wife and two daughters were able to emigrate to the United States in 2001, but Bayram was forbidden to leave until seven years later, when he rejoined his family in New York City. A decision on his petition for political asylum is pending.[28]

At age fifty-three, his greatest difficulty in learning English is the retention of vocabulary. "My brain is full," he explains. "If I twenty-four, twenty-five years old, okay, I can teach [learn] in six months English. But I were old. Vocabulary is hard. I not remember." Bayram's an activist—he'd scarcely set foot on the JFK tarmac when he helped found the Kurdish American Cultural Society— and he'd like to open a business, but he's hobbled by a lack of fluency in English. "I not good now in New York, in America," he says. "I need my life. Not only business. Need my life."

At the end of our interview, he opened his briefcase and pulled out a Turkish paperback novel written by—Bayram Karaca.

Funny . . . I pictured tutoring unlettered immigrants, and the IRC gives me an Iraqi chemistry professor, and at CELTA I get a Kurdish author. Americans look at these men and see people without positions, out of place, barely scraping by. They know that's how we see them, and they feel it. It's crushing. (And I think *I'm* suffering loss of status, because I don't get to ride big elevators anymore.)

---

28 Byron was finally granted asylum in October 2011.

Tuesday, December 1, 2009

Task-based learning: We watch a video of a British ESL teacher coaching a small class of adults as they plan a hypothetical tour of England. She begins with a receptive-skills (reading, listening) warm-up: Sitting with a picture book of England on her lap, she turns the pages and tells the students about possible destinations, using target language and functional phrases for trip planning.

My life passes before my eyes. I find the video profoundly depressing; it's so small-bore. Is that me, teaching a little class how to plan a road trip? Has it come to this?

After watching me conduct a class, Sophie, the extremely intelligent and sophisticated Brit who has succeeded the equally impressive Lizzy as my group's coach, critiques my performance. No matter how well I do, it's never good enough; she always finds lots to criticize. I must be careful to avoid too much error correction with my students, she has said. But my mistake today was too little error correction.

Thursday, December 3, 2009

President George W. Bush appointed me Secretary of Education. I reached out to the Republican minority of workers in the department. I valued everyone's ideas. But I faced losing my job if I didn't start wearing suits and fancy shoes and having lots of meetings and managing a budget.

Tuesday, December 8, 2009

Lizzy, giving us some guidance on professional development, suggests we go to teaching conferences and do webinars.

I hate the whole idea of webinars, starting with the word.

Friday, December 11, 2009

Muhie greeted me with a smile and warm handshake. "You are our happiness," he said.

We reviewed weather words—windy, very cold, freezing. Muhie and Suad very much wanted to know exactly when winter ends here.

I asked their son Ayass why they have Christmas decorations on their house—Frosty the Snowman in the window of the storm door, tinsel and lights spiraling up the banister.

"Everyone on the street has," he said. "We don't want to be different."

Thursday, December 17, 2009

CELTA instructor Abby gives advice on résumés and applying for work: We should say we have a "CELTA Certificate from Teaching House at St. John's University," which is true. It gives the impression that St. John's University has something to do with the program, which is false—Teaching House just rents space here—but it looks better than "CELTA Certificate from Teaching House at 101 Murray Street."

Should you put a photo on your résumé (or CV, as I call it, because I don't know how to type accent marks)? In the United States, no. For foreign jobs, sometimes they want a photo. "Japan is fussy. They want 'good-looking' teachers," Abby says. She makes air quotes with her fingers as she says "good-looking," but I think the term is quite literal and refers to the young women that Japanese businessmen would prefer. Not much I can do about that.

A page-long résumé is enough, Abby says. "You're not doing a chronological CV. Just include relevant experience." Thank God. But when you sit down and actually do it, you see that you can't just have parachuted in from Mars to become an ESL teacher. Where have you been? What have you been up to? Who are you?

Wednesday, January 6, 2010

Without a master's degree, I can't teach in a public school or community college, so I'm hoping to get hired by a commercial language school, ideally one of the subway schools—ALCC, Zoni, New York Language Center—that plaster mass transit with ads aimed at immigrants. I've sent out fourteen résumés and have received just one response, from Language Studies International in Manhattan. A European-owned school with centers around the world, LSI serves an international clientele, mostly young adults who want to further their professional or academic careers by improving their English—not exactly what I had in mind, but it's a start. They've invited me to come in for an interview if I'd be interested in being added to their substitute teacher list.

Thursday, January 7, 2010

LSI shares space with the Metropolitan College of New York on the twelfth and thirteenth floors of 75 Varick Street. I walk through a polished-brass and tinted-glass revolving door into a cavernous marble-floored lobby. Impossibly tall young models in high-topped sneakers, portfolios tucked under their reed-thin arms, stand in line at the rich mahogany security desk before boarding the very large elevators that will swiftly lift them to the advertising agencies above. This is the edge of Tribeca, a happening part of town.

Kerry Linder, LSI's director of studies, unlike most people making hiring decisions these days, turns out not to be a thirty-year-old. She's gray-haired, professionally dressed, and has some sort of European accent.

Kerry says she usually tells applicants to try again in March, as business is very bad. People don't want to fly to the United States because of terrorism, and can't get visas because of terrorism, and don't have money because of the economy, so enrollment is low. But sometimes companies send executives from overseas for one-on-one lessons, and when she looked at my résumé, my business experience really stood out. (Good thing I worked at Time Warner! *There is no such thing as a mistake.* I think I read a Hasidic tale by that name once; its point was that everything you do moves you along the path of your life.)

At the end of our talk, Kerry suggests I go down to the second floor and talk to Dan Manolescu, her opposite number at another school, ELS Language Centers.

"Could you give me his contact information so I can get in touch with him?" I asked.

"No, just go down right now and say I sent you," she replied.

Was this strange? It struck me as strange, but I went down and found my way to a windowless cubbyhole where Mr. Manolescu sat at a desk talking on the phone while looking through a pile of papers and carrying on a conversation with someone standing in front of him. He put all that aside for ten seconds, long enough to take my résumé and tell me that business was terrible and he'd have nothing for me.

Friday, January 8, 2010

Practicing the English words denoting family members, Suad tells me that her sister cares for their elderly mother in Baghdad. Suad talks with them every day by e-mail and Internet phone. Muhie explains that Iraqis consider it very, very bad to put a parent in a nursing home—everyone would talk. It would ruin the family's reputation.

My thoughts turn to my own mother, who spent the last years of her life in an assisted living facility. I visited her as often as I could.

Monday, January 11, 2010

Because I'm five minutes late leaving to teach my class at the International Rescue Committee, I happen to be home when Dan Manolescu calls asking if I can come in to ELS *today* to substitute for a teacher. *Oh my God, this is my chance*—but in an agony of regret I tell him that I have to teach at the IRC until 1:00.

"Can you be in at 1:45?" he asks.

Oh my God, think, think. The shuttle from Grand Central to Times Square, downtown local to Canal, walk—what, best case, thirty-five minutes? "Absolutely," I said.

"Busted!" I exclaim to my son Johnny, home on college vacation and playing video games in the living room. "I said on my résumé I know how to do this, this, and this, and that I have all kinds of classroom experience, and now I really have to *do* it, and I know *nothing.*"

My IRC class, usually just two or three people, today has seven, and they all have questions about our lesson on how to write a three-part essay. (Say what you're going to say; say it; say what you said.) I get out a few minutes late. Fortunately the shuttle is full of people, meaning it should leave soon, and the 1 train comes, and I'm in Dan's office at 1:40. He hustles me down the hall, hands me a book entitled *Advanced Vocabulary*, tells me to take attendance first, and leaves me to teach an advanced class for an hour.

The students include Abdul, a wavy-haired Saudi dude in a leather jacket who says, "You can call me Gangster"; and a young Japanese woman so brilliant that when I have no idea what the text might mean by "a reactive person," she volunteers, "Sensitive? Like, if you say some small thing to her she will have a big reaction? Like, 'You shouldn't come in late,' and she says, 'Why are you so angry with me?!'" I just talk as little as possible and have the students talk as much as they can, and they don't seem to notice that I'm not really a teacher.

When that class ends, I go back to Dan's office. He hands me a copy of *The Oxford Picture Dictionary* and sends me to teach a beginner class for the next hour.

Lacking a lesson plan, I launch a game of Twenty Questions. Among the most avid competitors are Bruna, from Venezuela, whose eyes I can't help noticing are actually *powder blue*; Aissatou, from Senegal, whose fire-engine-red lipstick matches her blouse; and Yuko, from Japan, who looks like an anime character with her black miniskirt, spike-heeled boots, two-inch eyelashes, and jet-black pageboy. Games are good; even sophisticated, world-traveling twenty-year-olds really want to win. The class goes well. These women laugh when I say something funny; they write down what I put on the board; they ask me smart questions (What is the difference between *bath* and *bathe?*). Who wouldn't love teaching ESL?

Dan asks me to continue for the next two days.

Wednesday, January 13, 2010

Just before the beginner class got started, the teacher I'm subbing for suddenly trudged into the classroom, dressed in a crummy gray T-shirt, looking disheveled and depressed. She'd stopped by to criticize me for failing to collect and keep all the family trees that the class drew yesterday, which she had never asked me to do.

The reality flooded over me. I'm doing a loser's job. I should be working for a magazine. I should be working for a foundation. I should be working for a company. I have done everything in my life wrong. I felt deflated and demoralized—until I taught the class. Aissatou and Bruna pouted and Gangster scowled when I told them that this was my last day.

Friday, January 15, 2010

Last night I was tired and figured I could put off Xeroxing pages of language exercises for Muhie and Suad until this morning. Mistake. I got to their house fifteen minutes late.

"We were worried about you," their son Tholfikar said as he opened the door.

"We worried about you," Muhie repeated, with a grave expression. "Fifteen minutes."

Tholfikar explained, "*Worried* in Iraq means 'check the morgue.'"

Later, Tholfikar's younger brother Ayass, who was a veterinarian in Iraq but is nothing here, told me that he has landed an unpaid volunteer job working the night shift at a veterinarian's office.

"That's great," I said.

"But there's no money," he pointed out.

"These days everybody works for no money," I said. "My wife works for no money." It's true; she does, very hard, as a social work intern at a school for kids with learning disabilities. "It's good. Maybe you'll get a job there, or they can be your reference for another job."

I focus on tutoring Suad, who needs to master basic survival English, but Muhie attends every session, and as the weeks pass the three of us grow closer. Still, I'm holding back one critical piece of information that they might take a keen interest in: I'm Jewish. I'd love to have a dramatic revelation and acceptance, a giant step forward for Muslim-Jewish relations, but I'm not ready to risk it just yet.

Today Muhie and Suad invited me and my wife to come to dinner over the weekend. I happily accepted, and we turned our attention to a lesson on doctor's-office vocabulary. I gave them a medical history form to fill out. It was a steep hill to climb; they didn't know their street address or phone number. Muhie took a well-worn piece of paper out of his pocket with a phone number on it, but they weren't sure whose number it was, theirs or maybe Tholfikar's cell. I dialed it on my cell phone, and the telephone on the table broke out in a merry rendition of "Jingle Bells." Go figure.

The last part of the medical history form asks for "ethnicity." I point out "White," but they choose "Other," and write in "Arab." Then Muhie asks me, "What is your ethnicity?"

Well, here goes: "I'm Jewish."

Suad fusses with her head scarf and says something to Tholfikar in Arabic. He translates for me: "She ask if you want your dinner to be kosher."

Not necessary.

As I was leaving, Muhie said to me, "To us you are Jimmy-al-azeez. Jimmy-al-azeez mean 'our Jimmy.'"

Monday, January 18, 2010

Read a clip from the *Times* about black pastors in Oakland building alliances with Hispanic immigrants.[29] When parishioners at Mills Grove Christian Church write Bay Area members of Congress to urge immigration law reform, they use letterhead topped with a quote from Deuteronomy: "Therefore love the stranger, for you were once strangers in the land of Egypt."[30]

Okay, we were once strangers in the land of Egypt. So what's your point? I should love the stranger because I wish someone had been there to love me when I was a stranger? Or because loving a stranger today will somehow increase the chances that someone will love me if I am a stranger in the future? How's that supposed to work, exactly?

---

29 "Trying to Build Bonds with Immigrant Stories," by Samuel G. Freedman, *New York Times*, December 26, 2010.

30 Actually, "the Torah [Hebrew Bible] tells us 36 times in 36 different ways to help the stranger among us," according to HIAS, the Hebrew Immigrant Aid Society, which now assists refugees of all backgrounds. (I tutored Soviet émigrés in English for HIAS a lifetime ago, back in 2002.)

Friday, January 22, 2010

Lisa and I had dinner at the home of Suad and Muhie with their sons Tholfikar and Ayass. Tremendous spread of roast chicken filets, fried chicken, meat wrapped in some kind of leaf, meat fried in rice batter; chopped lettuce, cucumbers, and tomatoes; hummus; red, yellow, and green peppers in a bowl; and a tomato soup with chickpeas and meat dumplings. Suad and Muhie apologized for the inadequate meal and crowded little dining room. In their Baghdad home they had a room for guests to gather in, separate from the private part of the house, because people routinely arrive unannounced and must always be welcomed in.

The chicken was fantastic; halal is the way to go. "This chicken is the best," I said, and raised my outstretched hand in steps—"good, better, best." Suad looked pleased.

We learned that Tholfikar had a job in Iraq as an operations manager for an American company that provided the barriers surrounding military bases. Their older brother, Suhaib, worked for the Iraqi embassy and was in the United States in 2006 when the rest of the family fled to Egypt, where they hunkered down with relatives for three years until the United States granted them asylum.

"We had every reason to be a target in Iraq," Tholfikar said. "I worked for an American company. My brother was in the U.S. My father was a doctor [PhD]. We were a big famous family in our town—everyone came to our house. Any one of these was a reason for us to be a target. We were threatened. They shot up the house."

On a lighter note, Tholfikar and Ayass told us they love *The Simpsons*, *Family Guy*, and *South Park*—especially the episode where Saddam Hussein goes to bed with Satan. Suad was a longtime fan of Oprah and Rachael Ray in Iraq, where people with satellite dishes pick up three hundred channels, for free. She asked her sons to ask us why the audience applauds when Rachael Ray says *cheese* or *garlic*. We don't know.

Their little sister, Farah, in jeans and a blue-and-white-striped polo shirt—no head scarf for her—arrived at 9:00 after her eleven-hour workday as a receptionist in a doctor's office and health spa. She told me I should be more strict with her mother, who, she said, does not do homework. Farah seems to think her sixty-year-old mother is refusing to learn English.

At the end of the meal no one would hear of us (or anyone else) helping Suad to clear the table or do the dishes.

Monday, January 25, 2010

Only Grisha and Rexhap, whose citizenship tests are fast approaching, showed up at the IRC. Grisha cleans offices overnight and cares for her husband, who recently had a heart attack, during the day, but somehow makes it to class faithfully. Rexhap, an ethnic Albanian high school history teacher who fled Kosovo in 1989, is a doorman at an Upper West Side apartment building. He worked all night and had to be back at his post right after class.

Rexhap—or Reggi, as he suggests Americans call him—is struggling with English. "I read New York *Times*, understand every word," he told me, "but speak, no." He can't write in English very well, either. He's at his wits' end trying to learn how to spell words with the long "a" sound. Should it be "a" or "ay" or "ai" or "eigh"? He hasn't been able to figure out the rules, because there aren't any. Reggi's citizenship test is just three weeks away, and often as not he spells the name of this country "United Staits," which isn't going to win him any points with the examiner. I showed him a $1 bill, pointed out UNITED STATES OF AMERICA at the top, and urged him to look at it every night before he goes to bed.

Wednesday, January 27, 2010

Went to 98th Street and Madison Avenue, down the block from Mount Sinai Hospital, to see how Saad Atwah from the Arab American Association is doing. I walked up to a steel cart with a blue-and-yellow Sabrett umbrella, waited for the man in front of me to pay, and said, "Two hot dogs, please."

Saad looked at me for a second, and then exclaimed, "Mr. Jim! Very good!" as he extended his hand to me in a broad, slow-motion gesture: Here is my hand; it will really please me if you will extend your hand to me as well. He's not just holding out his hand; he's holding out himself. As we shook hands he pulled me into a hug, pressing his cheek to mine and making a kissing sound. His cheek was scratchy, like my father's when I was a boy.

"Sit! Sit!" he said, pointing at a flimsy bridge chair beside the cart. "Hot dog? Mustard? Relish?"

"Just mustard," I said.

"Onion?"

"No, just mustard, thanks."

He handed me the hot dog, waving aside my hand as I went for my wallet.

A gruff man rolled up in a shiny black SUV, got out, and demanded, "Give me two hot dogs." As Saad served him I read the sign on the side of the cart: SABRETT HOT DOGS, GABRILA'S KNISHES, TOWER ISLE JAMAICAN MEAT PATTIES. Something for everyone.

It was a raw, windy day under leaden skies, typical New York winter. A customer came up every minute or two. None of them greeted Saad, and only a few said, "Thank you."

"Coffee?" Saad asked me, pointing at a cart nearer to the corner. He said something in Arabic that I could tell from the rhythm and tone must have meant that he knew the other vendor and the coffee would be free. I said "No thanks" and stood up to talk. Saad raised his voice emphatically, pointing at the chair. "Sit down! Sit *down!*" He picked up a knish and handed it to me. I dutifully took a bite. I can't remember the last time I ate a knish.

Saad pulled a $20 bill from his wallet and with a joyful smile and much excitement told me a story. "Man come, two hot dogs, no change, quick quick." He mimed a man running away. I asked if that happened today or yesterday. He didn't understand. The man in a Yankee hat selling children's books from a table between Saad and the coffee cart came over and asked the same question, pointing at the ground as he said "Today" and gesturing with his thumb over his shoulder behind him when he said "Yesterday." Saad smiled, pointed his thumb over his shoulder, and said, "Yesterday." Time as space.

The book vendor, speaking in a slurred and mumbling manner, said something joshingly to Saad that ended with the words, "your bullshit!" Saad laughed. If I couldn't understand the man's words, I can't imagine that Saad could either, but it's all about the intonation. A friend was ribbing him.

"Your wife is fine?" I asked. Saad said yes.

"Your son?"

"Mohammed at Buffalo. Doctor!" Saad beamed. With a few more questions I gathered that Mohammed's in college at the State University of New York in Buffalo. He's on his way.

To make conversation, Saad pointed east and said, "Madison." He pointed west and said, "Park ... uh, uhhh ...," trying to think of another word, shaking his head in frustration.

"Central Park?" I suggested.

"Yes, yes, Central Park!"

"Doctors," he said. "Hot [he mimed jogging]. Water. Soda. Mothers [he mimed pushing a stroller]." All of which to say, he's got a very good spot.

I said I would come again. I'm sure Saad understood that. We hugged again, twice.

Thursday, January 28, 2010
Got a call from Kerry at LSI. They need me to substitute-teach an upper-intermediate class for two weeks, starting Monday!

Friday, January 29, 2010

The head of People magazine offered me an editing job at $4,000 a week. I agreed to do it, but only until the summer. "I mean the summer of 2018," I joked.

Saturday, January 30, 2010
Dropped by the old apartment building where Reggi is a doorman, on West 54th Street, around the corner from the David Letterman Theater, to bring him a book on short and long vowels that may help him with spelling. He has to write at least one of three dictated sentences correctly to pass his naturalization test.

As I turned the brass knob, Reggi, wearing a navy blue jacket with the building's address in gold thread on the breast pocket, pulled the door open from inside.

Reggi is a big man, strong, with a crooked nose, milky blue eyes, and black hair gone gray and scanty on top. I always thought of him as depressed, maybe because he's far from his family and is no longer a history teacher, and to become a citizen needs to know more English than he's able to learn. Today, though, removed from the IRC classroom, site of his frustration, he hugged me cheek to cheek, smiled broadly, and seemed happier with himself, me, and life in general than I've seen him before.

He bade me sit down, got us some coffee, and told me his story.

An ethnic Albanian born in Montenegro, Reggi was teaching history in a high school in Kosovo when Serb nationalists embarked on their campaign of ethnic cleansing. Anyone who taught Albanian history or language was considered an Albanian nationalist and an enemy of Serbia. In 1989, he fled to the United States, leaving his wife, two daughters, and son behind. Just weeks after he escaped, 250 teachers were arrested, and 100 are unaccounted for. "Some say alive, some no," he told me. His wife warned him it was not safe to return.

In the United States Reggi asked for political asylum. A decade passed before it was granted, finally enabling him to travel abroad. "After ten years, I go to Kosovo," he said. "All Kosovo, it's finished. It's fire. I see my family after ten years. My father kiss me, kiss me, kiss me. I say, 'This too much. All my life you not do this.' My mother cries for half-hour."

Reggi returned to the United States so he could keep sending money to his parents, wife, and son. (His two daughters married and got out of Kosovo.)

As I sipped my coffee Reggi excused himself for a moment, unlocked a storage-room door, and returned holding two paperbacks. "My books," he said. "I write five." The first three were about the history of Albania, he told me. These were numbers four and five, a memoir of his career as a teacher in Kosovo and an account of his exile and adjustment to life in America.

"Do you sell these books?" I asked.

"Yes, very much," he replied. "Goes good. Half-million Albanian here."

Book number five has a picture of people marching behind a banner that reads MILOS ... HITLER; a photo of Reggi crouching with his hand on a gravestone, looking grim; and four pages of business cards from New York establishments run by Albanians, including several pizzerias and some well-known Italian restaurants.

Monday, February 1, 2010

Brooklyn Fire Victims Mourned in Two Countries[31]

By David M. Halbfinger

In Brooklyn, a Guatemalan immigrant grieved for his wife, killed after their tenement apartment burst into flames as they slept. His eyes red from sobbing, his hand stitched and bandaged beneath a new black funeral suit, the man could do no more than console his toddler son while waiting to see if his infant daughter would live.

Back home in the mountains of western Guatemala, three sisters who had heard about the fire on Saturday steeled themselves for the worst. By late Sunday, the worst seemed all but certain: Their three husbands, who had made their way to America together last year in search of work, all appeared to have perished in the same Brooklyn blaze.

As I was reading this story today, I wrote in the margin, "other = less than."

I'd become aware, for a moment, of an unexamined assumption, an attitude, really, a positioning or posture or vantage point from which I understand, in the sense of *accept* rather than in the sense of *comprehend*, that there are other people who are somehow less than I, and things like this happen to them.

No matter how sensitive the human interest story that I read (or that I write), there is still this gulf between me and them. To an extent, of course, *them* comprises all people who are neither me nor mine: people in the other cars on the highway; people in the other seats at the movie. But socioeconomic differences, skin

---

31 *New York Times*, February 1, 2010.

color differences, differences in stature and status—all of these can increase the distance between those beings and their pain, and the pain that is felt by the only feeler of pain who feels my pain, me.

I'm indulging in the sort of slathering of words across a page that the Latino folks in the tenement probably didn't have time for, but that they may have hoped their children could engage in someday.

Wednesday, February 3, 2010

My LSI class meets Monday through Friday, 9:00 to 1:00. Twelve hours under my belt—I've doubled my classroom experience.

The fourteen students—eleven women, three men, mostly Korean and Japanese, ages nineteen to thirty-three—are all well-educated and highly motivated, here on student visas to improve their English and boost their prospects. They're in my classroom because it's exactly where they want to be. How many American college professors can say that about their students?

Today Miyoung came up to me after class. She's the tiny Korean student who always answers in a whisper when I call on her. She'll speak up, barely audibly, only after I tell her she's right (which she always is) and ask her to repeat her answer. (Today she noted that two vocabulary words, *shy* and *reserved*, apply to her. "I have a hard time making friends," she said.)

"Jim, can I ask a question?" Miyoung inquired, standing in front of my desk with her hands folded. She extended her palm toward me. On it were a penny, a nickel, and a dime. "Why does the little coin not say 'ten cents'? The penny says 'one cent' and the nickel says 'five cents.' Why does it say 'one dime'?"

She recounted that she'd been trying to pay for something in a store, and the salesclerk said she owed ten cents more, and Miyoung couldn't find that sum among her coins. Finally she just held out her hand with all her change and let the clerk pick up the ten cents.

"Wow, I did not know that about dimes," I said. "When you are in another country, your eyes are open. You see things that a person who lives there doesn't see. This is very interesting." I could tell that the experience with the clerk had been embarrassing and humiliating, even though (or because) he had helpfully lifted the coin from her palm. "Welcome to the club of people who know it's called a dime and don't know why," I said. I hope I reassured her. I wish I could make her sad moment un-happen, but the only past I can affect is the one that's happening now.

I'm still hoping to teach struggling immigrants, the people who most need help, and I finally landed an interview yesterday afternoon with the New York Language Center. The branch I went to is a second-floor walk-up in the shadow of the elevated subway in Jackson Heights, Queens. I met with Anna, who I think runs all five NYLC facilities in New York, in an office barely big enough to contain her small, gray-metal desk and a folding chair for me. When she asked me to demonstrate how I would convey the meaning of the present continuous tense, I stood up to demonstrate "I am walking," took one step, and ran out of room.

"Why would you want to do this?" she asked, looking up from my résumé.

"First of all, it's like helping my grandparents. They were immigrants," I said. "And secondly, I got laid off."

Anna said she had no openings now, but she'd keep my file on hand.

Saturday, February 6, 2010

I'm looking at the lovely, friendly Japanese women in the class, and I'm thinking, *World War II—what was that all about?* Hard to imagine their grandfathers bayoneting babies in Nanking, or our dropping bombs on their cities, incinerating toddlers on playgrounds and mothers on maternity wards and children in classrooms. It seems completely insane.

Saturday, February 13, 2010

I love teaching. I'm exhausted at 9:10 a.m. and then totally alive and happy and energetic at 9:12, two minutes into the four-hour class. But then afterwards, the minute I walk out onto the street, I think, *Okay, I like teaching, but shouldn't I be teaching at a college? Shouldn't I be on a larger stage, doing something commensurately respected and compensated? Why am I working with twenty-four-year-old colleagues doing this as their day job?*

But really, the main thing is that I'm completely happy and absorbed while I'm teaching. Isn't that the main thing? My wife's friend Lynne said if I'm happy teaching and unhappy when I step out on the sidewalk, what I need to change is not the teaching part but the sidewalk part. I need to work on my sidewalk attitude.

Thursday, February 18, 2010

I started teaching on February 1, subbing for two weeks, I was told, but this is the end of week three, and no one has said anything. Today my students asked me if I would still be here next week. Aya, a nineteen-year-old who looks like a Powerpuff Girl with her freckles and exaggerated eyelashes, and Sayaka, a former pharmaceuticals sales rep who'd quit in exhaustion at the age of twenty-seven, looked positively stricken when I replied that I didn't know. I told them it would be my homework to find out, so I asked my boss, Kerry. She said that I can keep teaching this class for as long as I want, and that the bottom teacher mailbox is mine. She was surprised when I told her that I didn't have a key to the supply closet.

It seems that I work at LSI.

I'll have to resign from tutoring at the International Rescue Committee office, but I can still work with the Iraqis.

Friday, February 19, 2010

Two minutes after I sat down with a novel (*Brooklyn*, by Colm Toibin), the phone rang. "It's Nagrisha [something-something –ov]," a woman with a heavy foreign accent said. I spun the wheels of my brain. Nothing. "Do you know me?" she asked.

"Oh, *Grisha!*" I exclaimed—my student at the IRC.

"Yes. I am calling you to let you know that I took my citizenship test and I passed. And I want to thank you for your helping me."

"See what a difference you made in that person's life?" my wife said.

Monday, March 1, 2010

I'm in Colorado visiting my daughter, Halley, so I got together with David Worley, the dean of admissions at the Iliff School of Theology in Denver. He's the one who spun my head around at the Idealist.org confab last June, when he said finding meaning in your work may have more to do with you than the work. Worley, an under-forty guy with fashionably close-cropped hair, met me in his bright little office in the school's library/classroom/administration building.

"At the job fair in New York last June, you said that a lot of people come to divinity school looking for meaning," I began. "What are they hoping to find?"

"I think we have to talk about different models of meaning," Worley replied. "Certain people are going to find meaning in a transcendent form. They're going to conceptualize meaning as serving God, or something else that's transcendent, but for most Americans, that's 'God.'

"Another model is serving others in meaningful ways. We see a lot of students who have been in the legal profession, for example, come for a second career. Usually those folks are coming from the perspective of, 'I've spent the first two-thirds of my working life not feeling great about what I'm doing, and now I really want to do something that serves people.'"

(Typing this, it hits me that I'm spoiled and very selfish, wanting to have work that serves people. *I want, I want, I want* [as the voice in Henderson the Rain King's heart said].)[32]

"Then," Worley went on, "I think there's a third group of people who want to feel integrated and fulfilled. I think each of the categories wants to feel that, but I think for this third group it's not so much about the transcendent, or the need to provide something for other humans, it's more 'I just want to have an integrated life.' You'll find a lot of second-career folks are like, 'I worked in corporate communications my whole life, and I realize that I have this passion for early Christian history, and I really would love to study that more and potentially teach, if I can get a job doing that.'"

I showed Worley a clip from a *New Yorker* article I'd just read about Paul Krugman, the Nobel Prize–winning economist and *New York Times* columnist, which addressed the issue of finding meaningful work.[33]

"Krugman talks about what he does with his life, as opposed to what some other economists do with theirs," I explained. "He says he can't fly out into the boondocks and live on yak meat like the Third World development crusader Jeffrey Sachs. And he's not about to run Harvard University, as Lawrence Summers did.

---

32 In *Henderson the Rain King*, by Saul Bellow.
33 "The Deflationist: How Paul Krugman Found Politics," by Larissa MacFarquhar, *New Yorker*, March 1, 2010.

'I can organize my thoughts,' Krugman says, 'but I can't organize my office, and I certainly can't organize other people. You've got to figure out what you're supposed to be doing.'

"He says, 'Figure out what you're *supposed to be* doing,'" I repeated. "He doesn't say 'decide what you want to do.' And when you say 'supposed to,' it sounds like you're referring to some kind of directive coming from outside yourself, from something *out there*."

"Right," Worley responded. "I can introduce you to all kinds of people who would absolutely affirm that they believe that God has called them to do something in the world. Now I personally am not convinced of that, and that's why I really think that it's critical to know what your skills are, how you fit, and then to try to align your life as closely as you can. When I'm in that position, lo and behold, I feel like I fit better, that my life is more meaningful, that I am doing what I should be doing. From what Paul Krugman said, I think that that's what he's talking about.

"I don't think that meaning is somewhere out there in metaphysical space that one day clicks for us," he continued. "I really think it's a process of constantly working yourself into a better situation, and by that, I mean a situation that fits you better. You might find people that work for Goldman Sachs who think their jobs are the most meaningful jobs ever. It has something to do with not having to truncate yourself, being able to be fully you."

This young graduate schools admissions officer struck me as very wise, so I had one more question for him: "In June you said, 'To me the meaningfulness of what I do in a day depends more on the state of my centered spiritual practice than on the job itself.' What is *centered spiritual practice?*"

"Spiritual centeredness for me has been more and more about reminding myself that I'm going to be okay," Worley replied, "and that I'm not attached—now I'm starting to sound very

Buddhist—I'm not attached to certain outcomes that I think should happen. That what is, is okay."

I was grateful to Worley for explaining things so well. "You've brought *meaningfulness* down to earth for me," I said. "People think of *meaningful* as being synonymous with *significant, making a difference.* If you say you've found a meaningful job, a lot of people will think it's something along the continuum toward Mother Teresa. But *meaningful* also denotes 'making sense.' If I love working outdoors but I'm working at a desk, that doesn't make sense. If I align my work to my strengths and enthusiasms—this is what I like, this is what I do well—then my work makes sense; it's meaningful work."

Worley smiled. He liked my formulation. "That's a great pickup," he said.

I felt happy and relieved, as though everything was clear to me now, until, ten steps out the door, it hit me: If I simply redefine *meaningful* as a synonym for *making sense,* does that mean that any job that's a good fit for me is meaningful work? No. I've defined *meaning* down, that's all.

Something I read a million years ago came to mind: A teacher asks a little kid if he knows what some vocabulary word means, and the kid says, "I don't even know what 'means' means."

Friday, March 12, 2010
Nonmonetary Compensation:

1. After class, little Aya, looking like an M&M in her cherry-red sweatshirt, handed me a card with a bead bouquet and the words MANY THANKS on it. She's going home to Japan this weekend. On the inside, she'd printed DEAREST JIM in big, green letters, and continued in her meticulous handwriting:

I had a really good time with you. I enjoyed every classies :))
You're kind, friendly and you always take care of us . . . Also,
I think I want to be a perso who give many good influences to
people, like you . . . I really appreciate you!!
  Love, From Aya.

2. At my weekly visit with the Iraqis this afternoon, Ayass
    told me that this very day his mother had gone out
    alone for the first time, to the Key Food supermarket,
    and had communicated with the workers there. Hearing
    this, Suad put her hand over her mouth to hide her
    bashful smile and looked down modestly. "It close," she
    explained—just two blocks away. "Buy eggs."

Wednesday, March 17, 2010

I told the class this true story of what happened after our midmorning break:

I came in from outside as the last, most distant elevator's doors
opened. I rushed over and got in. I was the only one in the car. As
the doors began to close, I heard the clip-clop of a woman's shoes
approaching. I held the door for a long time, and when the woman
finally appeared, I said, "Are you going up?" She said, "No," and kept
walking.

"First of all, what *should* she have said?" I asked.

"No, thanks," the students said in unison.

"That's right, because I did something for her. How do you
think I felt?"

Sang, the sweet fellow from China: "Depressed?"

"Well, yes, sad, that's part of it, but I was feeling something else
more strongly."

Miyoung: "Disappointed?"

"Wow, you are much better people than I am. Yes, but the main thing I was feeling was . . . ?"

Karl, the suave Frenchman: "So what; let it go; whatever?"

I wrote on the board: "Pissed-off. Angry."

"Why?" everybody asked.

"Because I waited for her." I looked at my watch and tapped my foot. "I spent my precious time. Life is short."

I related this story to my friend Mike this evening. My point was that I'd learned my set point was much closer to rage than most people's.

"Well, in other cultures they are more passive, less inclined to anger," he suggested.

Maybe.

Friday, March 19, 2010

I see in the *New York Post* an amazing photograph of a swooping eagle, talons extended, about to kill a fleeing starling. This is while I'm reading *God Without God,* which says that God can be thought of as Ultimate Compassion. Yeah, right.

Tooth and claw—what a design for a planet! Everything based on killing, fear, and pain. Why not have all life live like plants? Nobody gets hurt.

Before I started teaching ESL, I used to think that Americans' avowed belief in the direct method, with the teacher speaking nothing but English, seemed suspiciously self-serving. Most of us speak only English, and it turns out to be best to speak only English in the classroom. How convenient! But now, with students from Japan, China, Korea, France, Germany, Russia, and Turkey in my class, I realize that no one could talk to all of them in their native tongues, so the direct method really is the only one possible. I don't have to feel bad about my limitations.

My country's limitations are a different story. Where my students come from, everyone learns a foreign language (English) in public school; medical care is free; the subways work; people don't dispute evolution or global warming. But in one area, we rule: popular culture. Defining the word *gossip* the other day, my students said, "like Brad and Angelina." There is no corner of the world where people don't know who Brad and Angelina are. And Jennifer.

Friday, March 26, 2010

I'm gaining an awareness of my own language. Yesterday I said that the (*tha*) and the (*thee*) are completely interchangeable, and Karl (the Parisian) exclaimed, "But there is a difference! You use *tha* before words starting with a consonant and *thee* before words starting with a vowel." I thought about this, talking to myself as I walked down the street: the cop car, the street sign, the sidewalk, the apple, the orange, the banana.

"You are right. Thank you," I told Karl today. "I can learn a lot in this class."

It occurred to me as I was brushing my teeth this morning that *unbelievable* never means "not believable," and *incredible* never means "not credible." That I had never realized how "tha" and "thee" are used was absolutely incredible. That I missed my subway stop yesterday morning and saw Canal Street flashing by was fucking unbelievable. But if Miyoung came in and said she had memorized every word in the dictionary, that would be not believable. And if a witness testified that he heard every word spoken by people fifteen blocks away, that would be not credible.

At class today Dahyun (my mnemonic: Only the good Dahyun) asked what the difference was between "made in" and "made by." I picked up a Casio electronic dictionary from the desk of the lovely Korean chemical engineer Ji Yoon (mnemonic: Ji Yoon bride) and asked the class, "On the bottom of this it says, 'made in'—where do you think?"

Everyone said China except our one Chinese student, Sang, who said with more hope than conviction, "Taiwan?"

"It's very simple, Sang," I said. "*Everything* is made in China." We all laughed, and Karl put his arm around Sang's shoulder. "You should be proud of that," he said.

Sunday, April 11, 2010

I WAS SITTING IN MY CAR AT A RED LIGHT, ADMIRING LILAC TREES IN BLOOM ON A HILLSIDE IN FLORIDA. I SAW MY FATHER WALKING DOWN THE STREET AND WANTED TO JUMP OUT AND POINT OUT THE FLOWERS, BUT I COULDN'T BECAUSE THE LIGHT MIGHT CHANGE. LATER, I RECOUNTED THIS TO MY FRIEND BRUCE. I SAID MY FATHER LOOKED SO HEALTHY AND HAPPY AND YOUNG; IT WAS AMAZING BECAUSE HE HAD BEEN SO SICK BEFORE HE DIED.

BRUCE SAID, "WELL, HE'S HAPPY BECAUSE HE'S GOT A JOB."

I SAID, "NO, HE'S RETIRED HERE IN FLORIDA."

BRUCE SAID, "YEAH. HIS JOB IS TO BE HAPPY."

I SAID, "THAT'S NOT SO EASY TO DO."

Tuesday, April 13, 2010

In class today, Ploy, the new girl from Thailand, asked what the little round sort-of caps are that she'd seen men wearing in New York, and also who are the men who wear big black hats and curls of hair in front of their ears.

I said that the caps were yarmulkes and the men were very religious Jews, and wrote on the board, "Judaism, noun = religion; Jew, noun = person; Jewish, adj."

"Lots of people are Jewish but don't wear those things," I explained. "You don't even know who's Jewish. Like, I'm Jewish."

Sachiko, our quirky Toyota heiress, gasped and exclaimed, "But Jews are geniuses, like Einstein! And Jews are really good with money!" She just couldn't believe it. Jim, a Jew, right here in this room! Everyone else laughed in sheer amazement at what she had just said. What else could they do?

"I know that you meant what you said with a warm heart," I told Sachiko. "Saying someone is a genius is a compliment. But when you say it about a whole group, it's a *stereotype*." We'd studied the word. "Why might I be offended by a stereotype even when it's positive?"

There was a rare silence while everyone thought hard about the question. I certainly didn't know the answer.

Miyoung raised her hand and said very quietly, "Because it's not you?"

On another tolerance note, I was pleased to hear from Sayaka that she cried when she watched the scene in *Glee* where the gay boy comes out to his father. From what I can gather, Japan lags behind the United States when it comes to recognizing everyone's equality; this was a big step for her.

Catching the rest of the class up on the TV show, I explained that *Glee* was about the uncool kids in a high school banding together and becoming cool. I put on the board, "popular, cool, uncool." Students suggested I add "nerdy" and "geeky" as "uncool" synonyms.

"Who's cool in high school?" I asked.

"Athletes," my young adults from Japan, Korea, China, France, Turkey, Brazil, and Italy replied as one. "Pretty and handsome people."

"Who's nerdy?"

"Students who do well in their studies," they said.

"In what field, especially?" I asked.

"Math," everyone said.

Who'd have thought that the same adolescent pecking order prevailed around the globe? It's a small world after all.

Wednesday, April 14, 2010

There are as many reasons to love my students as there are students. Sayaka is lovable because, when asked what she did last weekend, she said she sat in the park across from her host family's house and read a book and breathed the air and listened as a person behind her played a guitar.

Kotomi is lovable because in Japan she works full-time as a nurse's aide in a nursing home for the elderly, and she also volunteers nine hours a week as a nurse's aide at a facility for younger disabled people. Who works as a nurse's aide *and then volunteers as a nurse's aide*? And on Facebook, she lists her interests as "Chocolate, Jogging, Social Change."

"This is my last week," Kotomi said to me after class. My heart sank. "But I have decided to extend for eight weeks," she continued, "because I like your class. The class before, the rhythm made me sleepy. In your class I don't get sleepy."

I asked her to tell my boss.

Friday, April 16, 2010

Claire—she doesn't want Americans to even try to pronounce her Korean name—asked, "How can I say that I really don't care about someone?"

I wrote out the idioms "not that into" and "just doesn't do it for me," and led the class in an iambic pentameter chant:

I'm just not that into this school.
Jim just doesn't do it for me.

Then Flavio, our jovial Brazilian soccer player (left defender, Second League), *sang* the lines, helpfully demonstrating the rhythmic nature of English.

Tuesday, April 20, 2010

We were talking about the weather, as we do almost every day, because it's so important. (What else do people talk about? Sports.) I mentioned the word *clear*, and Jang, the anchorman-handsome Korean student who wants to be an anchorman, said it's what they shout in a hospital when they shock the patient.

The term *vice versa* came up in the textbook. To illustrate its meaning, I said, "I have no contract with LSI. They can drop me at any time, and vice versa." Miyoung came up after class and asked me, her big Keane-painting saucer eyes looking up into mine, "But do you wish to stay?" I said yes, but I was thinking that wasn't entirely true, since I'm trying to get a job at New York Language Center in order to teach striving immigrant hospital workers and night cleaners. It's going to be extremely difficult to leave. I love my students, and I love loving them, and I love their loving me—or, I should say, the me character I play at the front of the classroom—funny, engaging, patient, kind—nothing like I am the rest of the day and night.

Wednesday, April 21, 2010

Today we took a survey. Each student made up one question: "Do you believe in aliens?" (Flavio); "Do you like to drink alcohol?" (Ji Yoon); "Are you afraid of death?" (Kotomi). Six of the fourteen said they were afraid of death.

Friday, April 23, 2010

I rode the D train up to East Harlem for the farewell party for Jang, Sang, and Sayaka at Jang's apartment. As I watched all the local stations slide by—the D makes only two stops, while the B makes eleven—I was thinking that I remember almost nothing of my life. My four years with my first wife? A few scenes. Childhood? Forget it. I'm marooned in the present, the waters of time having risen and washed everything away.

Shoes were lined up at the apartment door, so I took mine off. (It's amazing that we Americans don't customarily do that, when you think about what's on the sidewalk.) Sayaka and Junko patted the sofa cushion between them, meaning *sit* in any language. So I sat down facing Jang and the monitor behind him, on which Lady Gaga was dancing as erotically as possible—distracting, but soon enough I forgot about her.

Sang was there, too, and Dahyun and Miyoung. We ate Chinese takeout—in a classic progression, the phrasal verb "take out" had evolved into an adjective (take-out food) and then a noun, takeout—and we talked about chance and love.

Junko, a corporate PR person from Japan, said that she'd bumped into a junior high school classmate on the street in Manhattan. She felt this was meaningful. I thought it was nothing more than one of those trillion-to-one coincidences that happen every day. We just don't notice them. What are the odds against us all being in this room together, people from all over the world? Virtually infinite, we agreed. (I felt lucky.)

Which is not to say that one-in-a-trillion coincidences are not important, I said. Nothing is more important than chance. One night when I was in college, I saw a tall girl with long dark hair standing in front of a dry cleaner on Broadway. I asked her if I could take her picture (so I'd have a reason to ask for her address—to send it to her). Long story short, we became friends, Jean and I, and ten years later, I set up my best friend with her sister on a blind date, and they got married. Then Jean's sister set me up on a blind date with a young woman named Lisa—who lived two hundred miles from me, but, hey, why not?—and we got married. So if I had walked past that corner five minutes earlier or five minutes later, two marriages would not have happened and my children would not exist.

Everyone has a story like that. Everyone *is* a story like that.

Life is not like driving—I mimed hands on a steering wheel—it's like—what are those games where the silver ball goes *bing, bing bing?* I couldn't think of the word.

"Pinball," Jang said.

The mention of driving led Sang, who's older, in his thirties, and apparently wealthier than the other students—most are here for a few months max, but he's taking a whole year's vacation from China—to ask a question about American traffic law enforcement. On a trip out to see his girlfriend in Ohio, where she's getting an MBA, he drove through an E-ZPass toll without an E-ZPass, because he was trapped in the line and couldn't get out. He wanted to know what fine to expect. I said I didn't think it would be too bad, that the one thing to really watch out for is getting your car towed from a tow-away zone in New York City, because it costs over $200 and a whole day of your time to get your car back.

"My car was towed away once in Beijing," Sang said.

"What did that cost you?" I asked.

"Nothing," Sang replied. "I called a friend and the police brought my car back."

Who *is* this guy?

Later, as I was putting my shoes back on in the narrow hallway near the door, Sayaka gave me a note, on a Salvador Dali card (*The Persistence of Memory*, Museum of Modern Art):

> *Dear Jim,*
> *I don't know what can I write at first.*

Because I have "millions of thanks" for you. Thank you for everything. Thank you for supported to me. You are super great teacher.

Do you know that how much did you teach me?

More than your think!!! Not only English.

I got a lot of energy from you and N.Y. Because when I quit job which call MR or Medical Representative, I was so tired. Now, I can do anything I want. When I go back to Japan, I have to think about a job and my future. Before I came N.Y. it means negative but now, it's possitive. I'm very happy to lived in N.Y. and spend times with you. I'm lucky girl!! I could meet you, make many friends, have a good time and speak English.

Thank you so much.

Sayaka

P.S. I didn't use dictionary for this!! Just I wrote in English!!!

Monday, April 26, 2010

Sayaka and Sang and Jang, in my class from day one, are gone. I feel bereft.

Thursday, April 29, 2010

It dawned on me last night why Sachiko looked so startled when I mentioned Goldman Sachs yesterday. Non-native speakers often hear and say short "a" as short "e," pronouncing *past* as *pest*. When I was talking about Goldman Sachs, she must have thought I was saying *Goldman sex*.

My students also struggle with the "u" in bug—they say it like the "oo" in book.

Thus, today's lesson: "Suppose that having sex with a person who works at Goldman Sachs is really bad," I suggested. "Then you might say, 'Sachs sex sucks!'" I wrote this on the board and had the class shout it in unison several times. They got those vowels right.

Friday, April 30, 2010

I'm not a big fan of Student of the Month awards, because I never got one, and they always seemed to go to teachers' pets or undeserving people whom I didn't like. But as long as LSI was going to give it to someone, I suggested Sachiko.

Sachiko is courageous. She suffers from a debilitating chronic illness—when asked to use the word *hardly* in a sentence once, she said, "I have hardly any hope that my physical problems will get better"—yet she always arrives early, always helps arrange the desks in a U and straighten them out after class, always participates in everything—and she got a 100 on her last test.

So, yesterday Sachiko stood briefly at the front of the room after the monthly school-wide pizza lunch as the director of studies bestowed upon her the Student of the Month prize, an LSI T-shirt. Sachiko was terrified of standing up in front of people, she told me later, but Miyoung helped her by holding her hand through the entire lunch. (One reason I'm so fond of Miyoung is that she always looks out for Sachiko.)

"I was crying yesterday with happiness," Sachiko said today. "I got a good-student award in elementary school, but nothing since. I called my mother last night, and she was crying too."

Wednesday, May 5, 2010

Re: body metaphors, "My heart wasn't in it" means you did a half-assed job, sloppy, without effort, I explained.

Jin Ah, a Korean girl who wants to be a journalist, steered me to a correction: "Does it mean you wanted to try, but you couldn't?"

"You're *right*," I said, having just learned something. "For example, I worked in business, but my heart wasn't in it, so I'm a teacher."

After class, Jin Ah, as usual looking vaguely delinquent in micro cutoffs and a gold Yankee cap, handed me a piece of writing she did on her own yesterday, asking me to correct any mistakes.

Meticulously block-printed on lined paper, Jin Ah's note began, "Today I met him who is my boyfriend to have a dinner which Korean food." Amazed by our weather, she continued, "Today's weather was little bit hot. Ha! I can't imagine Summer at New York. More hotter than now? Oh my goodness, I can't believe it." She made note of her studies ("relative clause is so funny, but little bit confuse to me. But I'll try to understanding this usage.") And then came the words that warmed my heart and prompted me to keep a copy of one page of the diary of a young Korean woman who'd come from the other side of the world into the room in which we stood:

> Happy May. Ah! Actually 5th May is children's day in Korea. So my father gave me a present, which is his KISS by phone. What a cute father! I love him. I wanna be children to him forever.

Friday, May 7, 2010

Sachiko is full of praise for Miyoung today. "Miyoung thinks she is plain, but I think she is eye candy," she volunteers, apropos of nothing, at the start of class. And, later, "I visited Miyoung at her working place, and in my opinion she is the best cashier in New York."

Julien, a young Frenchman, spills his coffee and mutters, "Oh, shit!"

"Did you just say 'Oh, shit!'?" I exclaim. "That's great! You're swearing in English!"

"Everyone says that in France," Julien confesses.

English is global now. Everyone speaks it, or wants to. We've won. Or should I say, they've won? The British, I mean.

Walker Lukens, the appropriately aged (twenty-four) ESL instructor and bearded folksinger who teaches the other upper-intermediate class, organized a scavenger hunt for our students on the High Line today and invited me to have coffee with him while they scavenged. (I noticed that rather than answer his Ss' requests for help with English terms on the hunt list, he told them to ask a stranger or figure it out. I should emulate him. TMTT is my weakness—Too Much Teacher Talk.)

Over coffee I confided that what I really want to do is teach immigrants, but I haven't been able to land a job doing it. Walker said that's what he really wants to do, too. "There's a moral hazard in teaching our students," he said. "They're all affluent. It's nice for them to learn English, but they're going to be all right no matter what."

At that moment I was thinking that he was using *moral hazard* incorrectly; it's the danger of setting a bad example by bailing out failed businesses or investors and thus encouraging others to believe they can escape the consequences of taking big risks. But never mind. I knew what he meant, and agreed with him. Only later did it dawn on me that we were wrong.

Sachiko, whose great-grandfather founded a parts manufacturing company that's a major supplier to Toyota, has traveled all over the world and is, it seems safe to say, quite wealthy. But she'd gone years without anyone telling her that she'd done something really well. And Sayaka, exhausted and depressed, had come to believe she couldn't succeed at anything. Maybe they were on a harder road than Saad the hot-dog vendor and his striving son.

Lesson for me: Affluent people are people, too. They can need help, and sometimes you can help them. You take your meaning where you find it, not necessarily where you expect it.

Thursday, May 13, 2010

This week I'm doing a one-to-one business-English gig for ELS, the school downstairs, tutoring an Argentine PepsiCo executive for three hours each afternoon.

Fernando is preparing to make a presentation in English to PepsiCo executives about leadership and teamwork (236 people report to him). He speaks only slightly imperfect English, using the phrase "have the possibility of" instead of "can," "could," or "might"; calling the ground "the floor," saying "this kind of things," "a person of your team"—tiny errors. Fernando told me the hardest thing he ever had to do was "fire" someone for poor performance who'd been his peer for three years. I taught him to say "let go."

Today he told me that PepsiCo's chairman and CEO, Indra Nooyi, says the company's goal is "performance with purpose," because, Fernando explained, "If we just make money"—he rubbed his thumb against his first two fingers, a universal sign—"what's it about? The PepsiCo Foundation is the largest foundation in Argentina. We support education for young people so they can learn a, a skill work?"

"A skill," I said.

"So they can learn a skill, so their children can have more opportunity than they did. We call it 'performance with purpose.'"

I nodded appreciatively, while behind my eyes I was thinking about Time Warner's mission statement and what bullshit it turned out to be, like Enron's, like all corporate PR. Fernando appeared to believe what he was saying. *He'll learn,* I thought. I was looking at a man at the tender age of thirty-seven, a man who still thought that he could serve God and mammon. You know what? You can't. You can look it up:

> No servant can serve two masters: for either he will hate the one, and love the other; or else he will hold to the one, and despise the other. Ye cannot serve God and mammon. (Luke 16:13)

I assured Fernando he's good to go. I hope he remembers me when he's king of the world.

Tuesday, May 18, 2010

Someone's heard that today may be a Jewish holiday, and the class asks me about it.

"I don't know what Jewish holiday it is," I admit. "I'm not religious."[34]

"I understand," Sachiko says. "I pray to ancestors. It's easier, because I never see God."

Thursday, May 20, 2010

Hani, a teacher sent here by her Israeli elementary school, sees things in English that I miss. After I explained what *bullshit* meant, she pointed out that the expression "shooting the bull" is simply a reversal of bullshit—*shit bull*—with shit toned down to shoot. Who knew?

Tuesday, May 25, 2010

In a lesson on money vocab, the Ss said how much they would like to win in a lottery. Jonah, a Swiss teenager, said $100,000, so he

---

34 A little research reveals that the next day, May 19, was Shavuot, which celebrates God's giving the Torah to the Jewish people.

could collect more CDs (music to my ears; I thought CDs were dead). Edoardo said $2 million, so that he would have a million left after he ran through the first million. Jin Ah said she'd like a trillion so that she could build middle schools and high schools in Korea. Kotomi said $10,000, "Because I afraid of money; money makes people crazy."

Sunday, May 30, 2010

Lisa and I go shopping for a new sofa. Ours is totally worn-out and would be a complete embarrassment, except who cares? We search in vain in four stores, assessing innumerable sofas—most of them so soft and deep we can't imagine how anyone could sit on them. I am thinking that no sofa we've seen, and quite possibly no sofa on earth, is going to make me any happier, and certainly not four figures happier.

On the way home Lisa plays a lecture about positive psychology she heard about in social work school. The guy on the CD recommends a happiness-supporting habit: Every day, write down three specific things you are grateful for. I'll think about it.

Monday, May 31, 2010

Today is Memorial Day, and Hani had a question: "I see everywhere there is Memorial Day sale, and people are going away on holiday. In Israel, Memorial Day is a very sad occasion. Everyone at a certain time stops. No matter where you are or what you are doing, you stop your car on the highway and get out and close your eyes and think of our fallen soldiers. Why in America is this Memorial Day, with shopping? I don't understand."

"Maybe Americans are stupid and shallow and selfish," I said, and asked the class, "Can you make a lot of money from people shopping and traveling and staying in hotels?" (They said yes.)

"How much money can you make from people stopping their cars and standing still with their eyes closed?"

"So it's all about money?" Hani said.

"I don't know," I said. "I'm just asking questions."

Saturday, June 12, 2010

Driving past the Verizon garage on Third Street in Brooklyn, I see, spray-painted on a wall by the entrance, HANG UP ON WAR. When I get closer, I see that it actually says HANG HOSE ON WALL. This strikes me as amusing, both because it shows how much of reality is created inside our own heads, and because, come to think of it, the two injunctions seem related: They both mean, realize that other people are centers of consciousness just as you are, and treat them as you would want them to treat you. Don't leave the fucking hose on the ground for someone else to pick up, and don't drop bombs on people, either.

Monday, June 14, 2010

With the Internet and Facebook and blogging and Twitter, I tell the class, real journalism and writing are suffering. Then I hand out a Xerox of this passage[35] and ask Ss to guess when it was written and what it's about:

> Now that anyone is free to print whatever they wish, they often disregard that which is best and instead write, merely for the sake of entertainment, what would be best forgotten, or, better still be erased from all books.

---

35 Which I took from "The Death and Life of the Book Review" by John Palattella in *The Nation*, June 21, 2010.

As I hand a copy to Nicole—the pint-sized Italian fashionista who admits to owning fifty pairs of shoes—she glances at it and says, "A scholar in the 1400s talking about the printing press."

"You looked at the bottom!" I exclaim. (The answer is upside down at the bottom of the page: Niccolo Perotti, an Italian scholar, in 1471, complaining about the invention of the printing press.)

No, she didn't. "I know everything about the past and nothing about the present," Nicole explains, "because in Italy, university study is very whole."

Tuesday, June 22, 2010

Ga Young informs me that in Korean, *jim* means "burden."

Thursday, July 1, 2010

Miyoung has decided that she's going to open an online vintage clothing store. "New York is paradise for vintage clothes," she says.

It strikes me that Miyoung's finding and selling cool old clothes is as meaningful as anything a person could do—bringing pleasure to people and new life to things.

Teaching these sweet, affluent foreign students, I've become less judgmental and more accepting of the usefulness/meaningfulness of all lines of work. Yes, it's wonderful that chocolate-jogging-social-change Kotomi cheerfully changes adult diapers in a nursing home, but it also seems wonderful that brave little Miyoung (from a land so male-dominated that abortion of female fetuses is still common, I read in *The Nation* today) scouts the world for vintage clothing and makes herself adorable in it and wants to provide it to others to make themselves adorable in.

Monday, July 5, 2010

The expensive new faucet set I found, through countless hours of online research, to replace the broken one in our kids' bathroom is a fount of perpetual pleasure to me. I gaze at it every time I pass by. It is graceful and shiny and strong—somehow *resolute*, I'd say—and built to last. Is this how people feel about their BMWs?

Wednesday, July 7, 2010

We read in the *Times*: A RECORD 103 DEGREES PUSHES LIMITS OF CON EDISON, which presented a new word, *venture* ("A record-breaking heat wave . . . tried the patience and resilience of anyone who dared to venture outside"), which led us to *adventure*.

"How does every adventure start?" I asked.

They weren't sure.

"The hero *goes*," I told them. "Like Ulysses. Like Abraham in the Bible—first word God says to him: Go. 'Go from your country, from your family and from your father's house.' And you've all done that. I admire you. I think you're great."

I mean it. Can you imagine being a nineteen-year-old Korean girl and getting on a plane to New York City where you know no one, to study English at some place you found on the Internet?

Tuesday, July 13, 2010

At LSI, I take my twenty-minute midmorning break—and finish the Frappuccino I've been nursing through the first 1:40—in the sunbaked sandlot on the other side of Varick Street. Encased in chain link, it's now the site of outdoor art installations. I'm looking at a 2010 work by Julieta Aranda called *Tiger, Tiger . . . (The Institutionalized Revolution)*, a nine-foot-wide oval made of horizontal slabs of white concrete on a pedestal, vaguely reminiscent of an old-style TV.

A plaque in front of it reads,

Television has the obligation to entertain those people, to take them away from their sad reality and their difficult future. I mean the middle and lower classes; rich people like me are not clients of television, because we never go out to buy anything.
—Emilio "El Tigre" Azcárraga

Yeah, I used to think that about *People* magazine, too. But, couldn't you say that about novels and theater and symphony? Couldn't you say that highbrow intellectual entertainment also serves the purpose of diverting us from our terror and sadness? The answer is yes; you can say anything.

Given that you can say anything, maybe the best one can do is to avoid making sweeping assertions like "Everything is bullshit" or "Life is beautiful." Take, for example, a bumper sticker I saw on a Chrysler sedan (the long, low model, named after a gun) on Baltic Street last night: WHY WORRY? GOD IS IN CONTROL. Holy shit, there's every reason to worry if God is in control. Wasn't God in control during the Holocaust? The Black Plague? Or maybe it just means, "What's the point of worrying? There's nothing you can do." In which case, why stick that on a bumper? Is that supposed to help someone make it through another day? I don't see it.

Wednesday, July 14, 2010

George Steinbrenner died yesterday. "I've been reading that he did a lot of good things," I said to Carlos, the young Hispanic lobby-security guard in an ill-fitting gray guard-suit with whom I exchange Red Sox fan/Yankee fan banter every morning.

"He was a good man," Carlos said.

"I thought he was a mean bastard," I replied.

"All bosses are mean," Carlos said, opening a window into his life.

Monday, August 2, 2010

I've never stopped calling the director of the New York Language Center, offering to teach anywhere, anytime. Finally, she's got a job for me, starting in two weeks. It's just two hours a night, four nights a week, for six weeks, but if they sign up enough students, the job could continue for another six weeks, and expand to more classes. This is my chance to teach immigrants, and I'm taking it, though I'll have to leave LSI.

"Why do you want to work with immigrants?" Junko asks me, after I share my plans with the class.

"Because they need help, and I can help them," I said.

After class I stayed for a while in the room, looking at it with newly appreciative eyes. Farewell to all this: Big windows stretch the length of the wall; the panoramic view to the north includes more blue sky than I'd ordinarily see in a month. (You can open the windows, but if you do and then someone opens the classroom door, a howling wind whips Min Hui's hair straight out like a flag in a gale, and it gets caught in the closing door if you're not careful.) Old Glory waves gloriously atop a tall pole on the corner of the adjacent building's roof, and beyond it, barges, tugs, yachts, the Circle Line, an occasional cruise ship, and once (Fleet Week), an aircraft carrier ply the broad waters of the Hudson.

If you walk to the window and look straight down you can see, right at the foot of our building, cars disappearing into the maw of the HOLLAND TUNNEL, spelled out in big block capital letters on a crossbar over the entrance. There is something stately and grand and *exciting* about it. (You've heard of it. *Here it is!*) And always there are giant outdoor ads, unfurled on canvas covering the sides of buildings, as though hung there explicitly to provide conversation topics for the class: This month, over a Range Rover grill emerging silvery clean from inky blackness, the slogan "Others Follow." Where to?

Thursday August 5, 2010

Reading *Gilead* by Marilynne Robinson. Page 49: "To be useful was the best thing the old men ever hoped for themselves and to be aimless was their worst fear."

Friday, August 6, 2010

My last day at LSI. At the end of class, I gave a little peroration.

"Thank you for being such a great class. You're great students, intelligent, energetic, and brave, getting on a plane and coming thousands of miles to New York City. The one thing I don't like about teaching is saying good-bye. But," and this had just occurred to me, "if I didn't leave today, you all would leave me, so I'm just beating you to it. 'Beat to'—that's a phrasal verb. It means doing something before someone else does."

I drew a time line from February 1 to August 7 on the board and wrote two sentences, one using the simple past, the other using the present perfect:

a.   Jim taught here six months.

b.   Jim has taught here six months.

"Which do you say today? Which do you say tomorrow?" I asked.

Jakub, the Polish teenager, got it right: b) today; a) tomorrow.

On the way out, I stopped by to see Kerry, the director. "Thank you for giving me the opportunity to teach," I said. "Believe it or not, no one else jumped at the chance to hire me. You must be very discerning, which is an extremely endearing quality."

"You can come back," she said.

You can come back. Are there any kinder words?

Sunday, August 15, 2010

I am grateful for the gentle cool breeze and the crickets singing at the Howard Beach A train station at 10:00 on a Sunday night.

There, I wrote down something I'm grateful for, as the positive psychology guy on the CD suggested. I should try to keep doing this.

Monday, August 16, 2010

First evening teaching at New York Language Center. The site I report to is located above a news store at 100th and Broadway in Manhattan. Everything about the place tells the students, "You are poor. This is all you deserve." You walk through a little door and up a sour-smelling, narrow stairway covered with gray rubber treads blackened with filth and held down at the edges with duct tape. On the wall is a large, faded poster showing smiling NYLC students. There are braces drawn over one student's smile, gum stuck to the forehead of another, a mustache drawn on a third. Would it be too much to put up a new poster? (And when I called the school today, I got a recorded message that said, "The school will be closed from December 21 to December 27. Enjoy the holidays!")

The classrooms are tiny, tightly packed with twenty-five battered chair desks.[36] It's impossible to arrange them in a horseshoe to encourage the students to talk to one another; impossible to put them in groups of three or four for discussions; impossible to let the students stand up and mingle; impossible to walk among the desks to monitor the students' work. I can't even write legibly on the board, which is made of some kind of cheap green vinyl on which chalk makes only a faint mark. All very unpleasant, especially

---

36 I'm talking about metal chairs that have a fold-down writing surface in place of an arm. I don't think there's a commonly used word for these things. Companies that sell them call them "chair desks" or "school desks."

compared to the luxe facilities of LSI. For this (and eight hours a week of me), each student is paying $200 a week.

I have thirteen students, all immigrants, twelve Hispanic, one African. We practice introducing ourselves and making small talk ("What are you doing these days?" "Not much. Studying English. How 'bout you?"), then turn to the textbook, *Worldview 3A*, and do a comparative-adjectives exercise that refers to brands of pizza.

"Teacher, what is 'brands'?" Dora asks.

The students have declined my invitation to call me Jim, and always address me as "Teacher." What could be better? Rabbi? That means the same thing.

"Toshiba is a brand of TV," I say. "Sony is a brand of TV. Panasonic is a brand. What is a brand of sneaker?"

"Nike," says Adam, the cashier from Darfur.

"Puma," adds Laura, the hotel maid from Mexico.

"Adidas," says Marilyn, the bookkeeper from the Dominican Republic.

There are no borders and no language barriers when it comes to brands.

Thursday, August 19, 2010

I hit the alarm this morning and lay in bed awakening, becoming aware of how tired I was, when, unbidden, the inner voice spoke up: "I can't believe I'm going to die, and disappear, and the world will go on without me, and it will be like I've never been. Fucking *unbelievable*."

Me, me, me. Stuck in specificity, circumscribed by the narrowest of limits, tightly defined. That's the whole problem. That's where the pressure and dissatisfaction come from, and the anxiety, the fear. All your eggs in one basket. Always here, always now. Me, me, me, me, me. That's the beauty of teaching. I escape into the eyes of my students.

After giving me a 100 percent positive written review, based on her unannounced visit to my class last night, my supervisor asked me to stay after school so she could tell me that she did notice one mistake. While practicing comparatives, my students said "Boys are more noisy than girls" and I didn't correct them, when in fact, my supervisor said, they were wrong. The rule, she said, is that −er is added to one-syllable adjectives *and two-syllable adjectives ending in an unaccented "y,"* so the correct comparative form is *noisier*. She even showed me a photocopied page from something called *The Grammar Book:*

> *When to apply the −er inflection and when to use the periphrastic comparative form* more *with adjectives and adverbs: First, adjectives and adverbs of one syllable take the inflectional ending, as do two-syllable adjectives with a final unstressed −y ending. [The examples given are* happier *and* noisier.*] Second, many other two-syllable adjectives that have a stressed first syllable and an unstressed second syllable ending in −ly, −ow, or −le also take the inflection, although it is certainly possible to use the periphrastic form in certain contexts, such as when a contrastive emphasis is being placed on the comparative element* (Ann is friendly but Beth is MORE friendly).

"Thank you for pointing that out," I said carefully, in measured tones.

Friday, August 27, 2010

Once in a great while, a computer at Time Warner e-mails me job postings for editorial positions. This came in today:

Staff Writer—TIME

We are seeking a talented and versatile business journalist to join TIME magazine and Time.com as a Staff Writer. This individual will be responsible for conceiving, reporting, and writing a wide variety of business and economic stories for the weekly print publication, several stories a week online, as well as daily blog posts about the prevailing business news of the day. A bachelor's degree and a financial journalism background, with at least five years experience at a magazine, newspaper or website is required. The ideal candidate with [sic] have an expertise and facility in producing clever, in-depth, counter-intuitive [sic], yet approachable stories about global economics, markets, technology, personal finance, company profiles and business trends—all on very tight deadlines. Salary is competitive. Clips and references will be required.

Hello? How can you conceive, report, and write "in-depth" stories for the print magazine while also writing *several stories a week* online *and* writing *daily* blog posts? It's impossible to properly report that many pieces, much less carefully consider what you are going to say and how you are going to say it. I guess when they say *in-depth*, they don't specify what depth, exactly—like, maybe, *shallow?*

Why not tell the truth:

Wage Slave—TIME

We are seeking a desperate, out-of-work writer willing to do the jobs of three laid-off employees for the pay of one. A high tolerance for slipshod work is required. The ideal candidate will have at least five years' experience of not caring anymore about real journalism. Ability to quickly produce and repurpose meaningless drivel on multiple platforms is a must.

Before class last night, Adam, the very tall, very thin young refugee from Darfur who wants to be an international competitive runner, said, "I have a question: How much English do you need to study for the GED?"[37]

I told him I didn't know; he should ask the people who run NYLC. But I really should find out. I want to be everything my students need, one-stop shopping. (When did that phrase go out of style in commerce and become just a metaphor?)

Thursday, August 26, 2010

Yefreisy, a teenager with a teenager's attitude, said something in Spanish to her friend Dora, a warmhearted Colombian housewife, and they both laughed as though unable to contain themselves, and did not stop when I stared at them. "English only," I reminded them sternly. I really didn't like their laughing like that. It represented a loss of control of the classroom; it made me smaller and them larger. But worse, it put me on display as someone who does not know their language, rather than someone who knows a language that they don't know.

Thursday, September 2, 2010

Tonight Ss wrote sentences using the past continuous and simple past, as in "I was watching TV when the phone rang." Dora read

---

37 General Educational Development certificate, commonly referred to as a high school equivalency diploma.

hers aloud: "I went to Atlantic City. I was playing slot machines and roulette when I won."

"How much did you win?" asked Julio, the fiftyish East Harlem jewelry store sales clerk, who's always chewing gum in an insouciant way that complements his sleeveless shirt and gold medallion.

"Two thousand dollars," Dora said.

"Can I lend five hundred?" Julio asked, chewing his gum a little more broadly, to indicate that he was joking.

This fortuitous exchange led to:

My Contribution to the Art of TESOL[38]

"That's wonderful. Thank you, Julio," I said. "Julio has brought up an important word."

I wrote BORROW on the board with an arrow at the top of the loop of the "B" pointing back toward the vertical stroke; and LEND with the bottom of the "L" forming an arrow facing away from the vertical stroke. I never thought of that before. Then I had the Ss make a giving-out hand motion while saying "lend," and a taking-in hand motion while saying "borrow."

Friday, September 3, 2010

Kotomi, after finishing LSI, decided to explore the Amazon in Bolivia for a month before heading back to Japan. That she knew no one there and spoke no Spanish didn't faze her—nothing does. She made it back to New York in one piece and came by today to visit Lisa and me before flying home to Japan.

At her request, we took her to visit a nursing home on Staten Island; she wanted to see if she could pick up any ideas for her own work. A nurse's aide there described for us what he does every day

---

38 Teaching of English to Speakers of Other Languages, a term that professionals prefer to ESL, because English may not be the student's *second* language; it's often the third, could be the fourth.

(turn, toilet, feed, bathe, walk, and speech-exercise patients), which is the same as what Kotomi does.

On the ride back, she told us that her work also includes some training of new nurses' aides, and she described one lesson she uses:

"Write down five things: your favorite music, food, book, friend, and activity," Kotomi began. "Now imagine you are very old, and you can't hear well, so cross out music. You have lost your teeth, so cross out food. You can't see well enough to read, so cross out book. Your friend is gone or far away, so cross out friend. You have nothing. So our job is to find you and bring you out.

"You use—" She wiggled two fingers at the crown of her head.

"Antennae," I suggested.

"You use antennae," she continued, "and know how a patient is feeling—maybe feeling bad one day."

At the end of the afternoon Kotomi gave us a lump of salt from the Uyuni salt lake in Bolivia, and we walked her to the F train on Smith Street. I hugged her as long and as tightly as I thought appropriate, and she gently patted my back as we embraced. "Good-bye," I said. "I'll see you in Japan or in New York sometime soon," and she said good-bye and headed down the subway stairs.

As Lisa and I walked away, I turned to look at Kotomi just as she turned to look at me. We smiled and waved and turned away.

Thursday, September 9, 2010

My boss at New York Language Center insists that she cannot decide whether I'll have a job two weeks from now until two weeks from now, when she sees how many people have signed up. And even if I do have a job, it will still only be four two-hour classes a week. So it was with the keenest interest that I interviewed at

LaGuardia Community College in Queens today for a job teaching a three-hour intermediate English Literacy/Civics class four nights a week. If I get my foot in the door there, maybe I can get even more work down the line.

Me, at a community college, where I thought you needed a master's degree? This is how the world works: A week ago, I encountered my son Johnny's friend Philip draped over a chair in my living room.

"How's it going?" I asked him.

"Pretty good," he said. "How're you doing?"

"I'm fine," I said. "I'm teaching ESL these days."

"ESL?" he said. "My mom teaches ESL."

"Oh, really? Where?"

"She's assistant director of the department at Brooklyn College."

"Your mother's *what*?!"

I called Philip's mother, and she told me that, while you need a master's to teach ESL to students *enrolled as degree candidates* at any of the City University of New York (CUNY) colleges, you don't need a master's to teach *adult and continuing education* courses. She immediately started forwarding me notices of openings for ESL teachers at various CUNY schools—an alternate universe heretofore completely unknown to me.

That's how I landed the LaGuardia interview—which I think I blew. A young man and even younger woman, sitting with me in the usual closet-sized office, asked me questions for an hour. When they asked, "How would you design a curriculum?" I sounded like I was winging it, as though I had never designed a curriculum before (I hadn't). I didn't even remember to say that I would include reading, writing, speaking, and listening. And when I talked about teaching with doctors' office forms and shopping circulars, I forgot to call the lessons "task-based learning" utilizing "authentic materials."

Damn, damn, damn. I wouldn't hire me.

Saturday, September 11, 2010

A beautiful, crystal-clear fall day, just like 9/11/2001.

Muhie looked pale and drawn. Ayass told me that his father was afraid there would be trouble because it's 9/11. "I tell him it's all right, but he's worried."

"It okay," Suad said, smiling and shrugging her shoulders. "Americans very nice, good."

"One in a hundred thousand—no, one in a million Muslims are terrorists," Muhie said.

"Osama enemy of Islam," Suad added.

In a fit of poor judgment, I showed them a story in today's *Times* about the controversy that has suddenly arisen over the long-planned Islamic community center near the site of the 9/11 attacks. "At first Americans said, 'Sure, okay, fine,'" I pointed out, "but then politicians stirred people up—to get power."

Suad agreed. Politicians appeal to "the low-down people with low mind," she said. She frowned and shook her head. They have seen where this can lead.

I explained as best I could that this cycle of hostility toward immigrants is an old story here. When the Irish came, Americans said they were lazy and stupid and should get out. Then the Irish became Americans and said people from Eastern Europe were no good and shouldn't be allowed in. Then those people became Americans, and they're angry—they think too many Spanish-speaking people are here. It happens over and over again.

Why is it always the people *inside* the castle who want to pull up the drawbridge?

Monday, September 13, 2010

Tonight we discussed our jobs.

Teenager Laura, very bright, best English in the class, works in housekeeping at a midtown hotel.

"If you don't mind my asking," I said, "do most people leave tips for the maids?"

Laura tilted her head in thought. "Umm, sometimes."

How often?

"I don't know," she said.

"Rarely, sometimes, often, usually?" suggested Jose, the pony-tailed young Mexican fellow who always wears black T-shirts and sits in the back. I was gratified to hear the adverbs-of-frequency lesson of a few days ago put to use.

"On checkout day, they leave five dollars," Laura said.

I always wondered about that. So, people do tip, but not much and most of them only on checkout day—which is outrageous.

Jose, up next, said he makes pizza at a restaurant on the Upper East Side. His classmates were impressed that he actually makes the pizza himself and asked if he throws the dough up and spins it. He said yes, but added out of modesty that he makes pies only up to fifteen inches.

"Is it easy to learn to make pizza?" asked Sergio, who works in a Fairway supermarket bakery department. He used today's vocabulary—adjectives grouped under Easy and Difficult.

"It's hard," Jose replied. He said he'd been working there for two years before he started making the pizza on his own.

These are exactly the people I want to be teaching. I feel terrible about possibly bailing on them to go to LaGuardia Community College, even though I'll be teaching immigrants there, too.

Wednesday, September 15, 2010

This evening I walked around pressing a cucumber to my students' foreheads as they worked through the "as/as" game: sort ten words into two lists—adjectives: cool, dry, good, strong, white; nouns: gold, bone, ox, sheet, cucumber. Then divide into two teams and send someone up to the board to match the words.

Yefreisy strode forward confidently and drew a line from "as good as" to "a bone."

"No!" shouted Jose and Marilyn on the other team. Yefreisy took this in good humor, smiling as she went back to her seat. "Good guess," I said, slumping against the wall and dangling my arms as though boneless. "Bones are good—but no. Anyone else?"

Adam raised his hand and walked up. He drew the line from "as cool as" to "cucumber."

"Right," I said. "But we don't walk outside and say 'It's as cool as a cucumber.' It means 'really calm under pressure.' Like, Cesar does food preparation. They bring out a pile of vegetables *this high*, up to the ceiling, and they say, 'You have ten minutes to do all this.' And everyone else is running around saying, 'Oh my God, oh no, we can't do all this, there's not enough time!' But Cesar is *cool as a cucumber*. He just does it; nothing bothers him." Cesar, smiling broadly, nodded his head as I described this imagined scene with him in the starring role. Adam got all the rest right.

When we had five minutes left, I said we had one more piece of business. "It says on the sign-up sheet for the next six-week session, 'Instructor—Jim Kunen.' That's not right. I'm not going to be your teacher." The class fell silent. "I got a call at four o'clock this afternoon offering me a job at LaGuardia Community College. I haven't told *them* yet." I pointed my thumb over my shoulder toward the NYLC administrators' office. "It's more steady and more hours a week. Here they only give me eight hours. That's not enough. I'm very sad to leave, because I love you all." I was a little surprised to hear that word come out of my mouth, but they seemed to take it in stride; it made sense to them. And it was true.

IV. This Is Now

I wish you what may sound like two things but is really one. I wish you a happy and a useful life.

—Professor Herbert Peterfreund,
NYU School of Law,
addressing his Evidence class
on the occasion of his retirement

Thursday, September 23, 2010

My first night at LaGuardia.

Located in Queens, where half the 2.3 million residents were born in another country, LaGuardia calls itself "The World's Community College." It's certainly big enough to be, with 17,500 students enrolled in courses for credit and more than 40,000 in adult and continuing education programs.

In Building C, the vast industrial structure where my class meets, three or four parallel hallways that may once have served as runways for light aircraft are crossed by an indeterminate number of slightly less lengthy corridors. All of these avenues are white-walled and fluorescent-lit, inducing a sort of snow blindness. There are occasional landmarks, such as a couple of old wooden court-house benches sitting incongruously against the wall of a gleaming hallway, but these can be found in *more than one place*, and, of course, can be encountered from several different directions, so that I never know where I am, and, what's worse, *never will*. Even the red penis picture (one of several large paintings of nude men and women interacting more or less violently in primary colors) isn't much help to me. I can't remember whether the penis points toward the main office (C-250) or toward my supervisor's office (C-233)—or does it point *away* from one of those places? Thank God, there are signs listing the random room numbers that can be found in any given direction at each intersection, so I always reach my destination, eventually.

Our classroom is shaped like a shoe box, only fifteen feet separating the blackboard from the back wall, while the students' seats range far off to my left and right. Once again, the CELTA ideal of arranging desks in a horseshoe so that students face one another is impossible. Through the open windows at the far end of the room comes the insistent racket of passing trains: *tickety tickety TACK! TACK! tickety tickety TACK! TACK!* I ask the Ss if we should close the windows. Everyone says no, it would be too hot. It occurs to me that some of them may live beside the tracks, so I avoid saying that the noise is horrible.

I put my twenty-four Ss in pairs, and after chatting briefly, each introduces his or her partner to the class. They're mostly in their thirties and forties: a hotel housekeeping supervisor, two home health attendants, a waitress, several babysitters and cleaning women, a janitor, a construction laborer, a painter—nineteen women and five men. Almost all of them say their goals are to improve their English and get a better job and become a U.S. citizen. (Only three of them are citizens now.) They've been on a waiting list for a year and a half to take this free class.

Lesson No. 1: I instruct everyone to leave the room and find two nearby fire escapes; return and write down precise directions to them; then exchange directions with another student and see if you can follow them.

When the students get back, a man in the front row raises his hand and says, "Fire escapes are black metal outside the building. These are not fire escapes."

Damn. "You're right," I concede. The words slowly come to me: "I think they're called fire stairs. You see," I point out, taking in the class with a sweep of the hand, "I learn from you." I have shown them at the outset that their teacher is humble and collaborative, or maybe just not very bright.

We turn to the textbook lesson on quantifiers: None of us, one of us, a couple of us, a few of us, some of us, many of us, most of us, all of us. Ss want to know whether "a few" means three, or could it be four? How about five? What percentage marks the transition from "some" to "many," and from "many" to "most"? This is very tricky. Getting the "most" votes can mean the bare majority, or even plurality, in an election. But at other times "most" means "nearly all," as in "Most birds can fly."

Most of us are native Spanish speakers; in fact, almost all of us: twenty-two Spanish, one Chinese, one Polish, one English (me).

Saturday, September 25, 2010

On an exercise bike watching TV, I see the beginning of an American Express ad, animated icons of happy trees and houses, with an earnest male voice-over: "Maybe you want to replant a forest. Maybe you want to build homes for those in need . . ."

I flip off the TV. I think I know where this is heading: American Express is inviting me (guilt-tripping me—remember that phrase? Remember guilt?) to donate my Membership Miles to charity. I don't want to. I've collected thousands of them, one for each dollar spent over many years, hoping to one day fly free to Australia. Let's not go overboard. I'm not going to give away everything I don't need, just to help other people.

Sunday, September 26, 2010

11:00 a.m., Iraqis' house.

"We have had a scientific experiment," Muhie says. "We have had Jimmy here, and we have had weeks without Jimmy here, and we have found it is much better when you are here. This proves that you are very dear to us." Nice to hear on a Sunday morning.

A little later, when Suad as always jumps up and says, "I make tea," Muhie launches into a description of a book he is writing. "When a man dies, no application of energy can make him alive, not electricity, not magnetism. This is the special energy of the soul," he says, nodding for emphasis. "Matter and energy are not different. Einstein calculated—"

"E equals MC squared," I interject, stealing his thunder because it's so important to me to show that I know, but Muhie pays me no mind and is writing $E = MC^2$ on a napkin when Suad comes back and sits down. She looks at Muhie with a weary, patient affection. I can tell she is thinking, *Here he goes again. But it's good for him. He needs this.*

"You have job, you not come," Suad says, when she can get a word in, meaning that I should surely stop coming now that I have the LaGuardia job, because her family doesn't want to burden me in any way.

"It's just a part-time job," I assure her.

"Part-time," she repeats. She knows what that means. To live in America now is to know what *part-time* means.

She asks Muhie to ask me if I teach children or adults.

"Adults, fortunately," I reply, "because you don't have to say, 'Sit, be quiet.'" I add that I love children—but not to teach.

"I want grandchildren," Suad says, flawlessly pronouncing *want*, which I enthusiastically commend her for. (She had been pronouncing it "went.")

"Who is the little boy in the picture on your computer screen?" I ask.

"That's Cookie, our grandnephew," Muhie answers. "He is three years old."

Suad corrects him. "Now he is big boy, he is not Cookie. He is Ahmed."

(Ahmed!!!)

"In Iraq we say, 'Children are the love of God,'" Muhie says.

As I walk to the subway later, I think of Muhie and Suad and Cookie, and then I remember what *New Republic* publisher Martin Peretz wrote recently: "Muslim life is cheap, not least to the Muslims themselves."

What an ignorant, loathsome creature he must be.

Friday, October 1, 2010

I've invited Adam to come to my house on Sunday morning. He told me in class at NYLC that he needed to study more English before he could take the GED exam, so I offered to tutor him. It seemed the least I could do for a refugee from Darfur.

Booray Adam Nour (*Nour* means "light," he says proudly) was seventeen when the Janjaweed attacked his village. As he and his family ran for their lives, two of his brothers were killed.

Adam's five sisters and his mother and father, a businessman who imported clothing and shoes from Saudi Arabia, have found safety in Khartoum, living on funds that his two surviving brothers send them from Saudi Arabia. Adam was able to get hold of a Kenyan passport, and in December 2008 he flew from Chad to Dubai. From there, he flew to Russia, then to Cuba, then to Guatemala, Mexico, and finally Texas, where he was granted asylum in October 2009. In June 2010, Adam came to New York City, where he moved into a small two-bedroom apartment in a housing project with a Sudanese cab driver and an American man, and then he found his way to the shabby little classroom where I turned up.

Now I'm worried. What if Adam comes to my house, is overwhelmed by our relative wealth and the absolute injustice of it all, and talks to another refugee about it later, and they get to thinking and decide they should come back under cover of darkness and break in and steal stuff? And maybe they should kill us while they're at it, because that way we can't identify them to the police, and anyway, we deserve to die, because we go about our lives of luxury while their families are slaughtered in Sudan, and we are so uncaring that we're complicit in that evil. Anyway, maybe they don't need a reason to kill; it's just what people do. It's been done to their families. They're used to it.

This is a paranoid fantasy. Adam is the sweetest young man I've ever met. There is something about his bashful smile when you praise him that is the incarnation of gentleness. I don't know how he does it. Where is the bitterness? The fear? The need for retribution? All he wants is to study hard and learn English and become a nurse. A nurse! He was born to be a nurse.

But. The son of the former CEO of Time Warner was a New York City public school teacher. He chose to teach inner city kids rather than glide into a lucrative corporate career. He loved his students. He helped them after school. He invited them to his apartment. And one day a few of them came and tied him up and killed him, then went and used his ATM card to withdraw some cash. There's a paranoid fantasy for you—except it happened.

Well, what are the odds? I could meet Adam in a restaurant, but then we wouldn't be able to study very well. I think I know him. Let's do it.

Sunday, October 3, 2010

Adam is due at 11:00. At precisely 11:00, he rings the bell. He responds to my welcome by gently placing his hand in mine, steps inside, and lights up my home with his beatific smile.

Sitting side by side at the dining room table, we open the Kaplan GED prep book I bought yesterday and begin what I'd planned on being a ninety-minute session. I look up at the clock, and it's two and a half hours later; we've done enough for one day. Adam will come back every two weeks.

Monday, October 4, 2010

My LaGuardia students wrote brief autobiographies over the weekend:

> *My name is Carlos. I am from Argentina. I came to the United States on Feb. 17th 2001. I remember it was Sunday. The next day I started work because I was contract with a company construction. I am a painter. I worked 7 days a week. I had a good salary. It was a good year but always missed my family. My family is in Argentina, wife, two sons and two daughters and three grandson. I continue to miss they. Every days I call my family. Sometimes I see they in the computer.*

Victoria:

I come to New York in February 2005 in Valentene Day. I come to this country because, to make a home with my husband. My husband work at company, He is handyman. He had wanted to work here and not longer be separated. He traveled to Peru three times a years and tol me to come, well he could love more and leave my work at the hospital, my family and friends. My parents and my sibling live in Peru. I call my family four day by week. I work full time in Great Neck Long Island all week. I clean the house. Saturday and Sunday is my days off, but Saturday I clean my apartment and I do the laundry. I am nurse in Peru. I miss my job. I got many dreams remain dreams. I want to learn English and in future performance as a nurse.

The amazing thing is that Victoria is not embittered, not discouraged. She is lovely, friendly, quick to smile. I could learn a lot from her.

Friday, October 8, 2010

They asked me at the job interview if I'd ever devised a curriculum. Now I know why: They don't give you one. They just lay out broad parameters: In an English Literacy/Civics course, you provide instruction in the basics of U.S. history and government to help students become informed citizens and active community members, and then you cover stuff like financial literacy and health literacy, to help them live and work safely in New York. For the English part, you set language-development goals, like, they're going to learn to form questions and use the past continuous tense.

The resource room had eighteen copies of one intermediate grammar text, *English in Action 3*, which looks good to me, because it's aimed specifically at immigrants, with the grammar lessons embedded in content about getting a job, renting an apartment, and so forth. That book plus authentic materials (maps, menus, catalogs) should cover the English literacy part. For the rest, there must be stuff online. We have to spend an hour and a half a week in computer lab, anyway.

Monday, October 11, 2010

Told the class we're going to study financial literacy (taxes, banking, credit cards, payday loan scams); government (they'll write to their city, state, and federal representatives); health and nutrition; and their choice of workers' rights, housing rights, or police and the courts. They voted for workers' rights, twenty-three to one.

Thursday, October 14, 2010

"You may not pay attention to politics," I told my students, "but politics pays attention to you." They knew what I meant; it's hard to miss the demonization of immigrants. We're going to keep an eye on the gubernatorial election campaign.

Tonight, we read "Paladino: Prison Dorms for Welfare Recipients" by AP writer Beth Fouhy: "Republican candidate for governor Carl Paladino said he would transform some New York prisons into dormitories for welfare recipients, where they would work in state-sponsored jobs, get employment training and take lessons in 'personal hygiene.'"

That's all Carlos, the painter from Argentina, needed to hear. "They no work," he said angrily. "Lazy."

I was surprised, but shouldn't have been. I'd figured immigrants would be put off by a reactionary politician's attacks on the poor, but my students work, and work, and work, and some are ready to be angry at anyone they imagine to be getting money for free.

Monday, October 18, 2010

Per an exercise in our grammar text, I asked the class what they would do for work if they could have any job in the world.

"Same as now," Carlos said. "I love my job. I am painter for thirty-eight years."

Christian, a round-faced young man from Ecuador who is often bored and not shy about showing it, said, "Restore antique furniture. I do it now."

"Doctor," said Marisol, a handsome woman in her fifties.

"What kind?" I asked.

"Pediatrician," she replied. "I was in my country, Venezuela."

Being an immigrant is like jury duty; you mix with people you never otherwise would. My students are from every social class, but so far as I can tell, they don't sort themselves that way; they tend to sit with one another according to their English ability.

Marisol, it turns out, was a pediatrician in Venezuela before she ran afoul of the Hugo Chavez regime, but there is no discernible distinction in manner or speech between her and the hotel maids and fast-food workers in the class (who themselves may have held loftier positions in their homelands). A lack of fluency in the language is a great leveler.

Tuesday, October 19, 2010

A huge Con Ed vacuum truck is cleaning out a manhole just down the street from my window. It sounds like the *Psycho* shower scene played against the background of a 747 taking off. I have a strong sense of grievance. This is not fair. I have done nothing to deserve this. It should not be happening.

A fucking truck is shrieking and roaring outside, I'm thinking. *It's always something.* But *what?* I might be saying, "The fucking Janjaweed have come back to kill us," if I lived in the village of

Adam Booray (who improbably sits at my dining room table on Sundays studying for the GED). Things are rough all over.

Thursday, October 21, 2010

Pointed out to my Ss that some words sound like what they mean. The class, in unison, read aloud from *King Lear*:

> *Such sheets of fire, such bursts of horrid thunder,*
> *Such groans of roaring wind and rain, I never*
> *Remember to have heard.*

Then I showed the thunder-and-lightning-riddled trailer for the 1931 Boris Karloff *Frankenstein,* and asked if anyone had seen the movie. No one had.

"I read the book," said Carolina from Colombia, now of Queens.

I haven't read the book. Meet the well-read, immigrant night-shift diner waitress.

Thursday, October 28, 2010

National Public Radio broadcast an investigative report this morning revealing that Corrections Corporation of America, which is in the business of running prisons for profit, has been aggressively lobbying for—and in some cases actually writing—laws that greatly increase the number of immigrants who are detained and incarcerated. According to company reports reviewed by NPR, "executives believe immigrant detention is their next big market."

I wish I could bring these Corrections Corporation executives to my class. Maybe if they actually met some immigrants and saw that they were thinking, feeling human beings, the executives would change their vile and violent ways. But they probably wouldn't give a shit. "It's business," they'd say, like they always do, as though it were an incantation that could purify a putrid heart.

Friday, October 29, 2010

At the "Nuts and Bolts" teacher-training workshop at the City University of New York Adult Literacy Program, they say every lesson plan should include four things:

1. English for Everyday Life

2. Relevant Topics and Themes (like nutrition, financial literacy, workplace rights)

3. Community Services and Resources (like where to get health care)

4. Learners as Experts (chances to talk about stuff they know)

"Marry rich language opportunities to these four categories to build a lesson plan," the teacher trainers say.

It isn't easy to teach ESL as well as it can be taught.

Wednesday, November 3, 2010

A couple of women from the New York City Commission on Human Rights came in to teach about workplace rights. Their lesson culminated in a quiz:[39]

---

39 The lesson and quiz were based on information in *The Right to Work: Understanding Immigrant Employment Rights, A Workbook for ESOL Classes, 2010–2011 Student Edition,* [by] NYC Commission on Human Rights and New York Immigration Coalition.

True or false:

1. An employer can decide to hire only U.S. citizens. (**False!**)

2. If you file a complaint against your employer for discrimination, your employer cannot retaliate against you. (**True!**)

Fill in the blanks:

3. Can an employer fire you right away if your Social Security number doesn't match government records? (**No!** Your employer has to give you a chance to prove your identity and work authorization.)

4. If an employer doesn't pay you, who should you call? (**The New York State Department of Labor.** If you're not authorized to work in the United States, an employer is not allowed to hire you. But if an employer does hire you, you must be paid for any work that you have done.)

I think it's safe to say that everyone in the room knew that the real world doesn't necessarily go by the book.

Still, I think it's good to know your rights. It's good to know when your boss is breaking the rules, even if you can't do anything about it. If you know what your rights are, you can at least picture a world where your rights are enforced, where you get what you deserve. It's a start.

As Marlene, a hotel housekeeping supervisor, wrote,

> *This class was very very interest. Because I know many thing abaut the descrimation. And ahora I know where go to for complain about people have problem discrimination. Thank for this.*

Thursday, November 4, 2010
This was Carlos's last class; he's leaving to take a painting job on a big project in Boston. He asked me to stand with him for a picture. As he smoothed the scraggly strands of shoulder-length, rust-colored hair emerging from under his baseball cap, I put my arm around his shoulders. They felt like rocks—all that overhead painting.

"Come visit us sometime," I said, as he headed out the door.

"Good-bye," Carlos said. "I see you"—he hesitated—"whenever." And he walked away.

Tuesday, November 9, 2010
National Public Radio is discussing Bush's presidential memoir, just out. That George Bush, the swaggering, entitled preppy two years ahead of me at Andover, that he became President of the United States, this is when reality went off the rails for me. This petulant jerk starts a war that kills untold thousands of people— and he's in a position to do so because a woman in Florida badly designed a "butterfly ballot" (a butterfly flapping its wings causes a hurricane)—this is too absurd, too far-fetched, and too horrible to be true. Unfortunately—and shame on me for not grasping this sooner—nothing is too absurd, too far-fetched, and too horrible to be true.

And meanwhile, I am a person of no consequence, doing unremarked and unremarkable things on a very small scale. I'm shaking my head in wonder.

For a computer lab exercise, I've typed out the directions students need to follow online, in order to find out where they can get free flu shots:

Go to NYC.gov

Left button: Drag to "HRA"

Right side: Select last line, "Health Insurance Access"

Left side: Select "Health-Care Resources for the Uninsured"

Center: Find "Available Health-Care Resources"

Click "DOHMH Clinics" for free flu shots

Back arrow: Click "Community Health Centers" for low-cost care

Thursday, November 18, 2010

I'm looking at the Latin Americans in my class and thinking about conquistadors and Incas and Mayans five hundred years ago, and here these people are with bronze skin and raven hair and regal cheekbones, speaking Spanish. It's strange, how the world works.

Tuesday, November 23, 2010

When I go out for my seven-minute walk each a.m. before sitting down at my desk, I always see two or three young moms pushing their toddlers in strollers along Clinton Street on their way to or from Cobble Hill Park. The mothers walk with strength and ease and confidence, paying no mind to the uneven sidewalks. The toddlers lounge in their strollers like little pashas, gazing serenely at the passing scene. Sometimes the little ones and I make eye contact, and I wonder whether my eyebrows raised in greeting or, more likely, my mustache and unanticipated gaze make an imprint that will remain forever in their brains like a fossil footprint in the mud; whether my face will appear in their dreams sometime, cast in the role of someone they know but don't know, or maybe a teacher who springs an exam in a course they'd forgotten they'd enrolled in.

But these days mostly I picture the toddler as an adult visiting his fading mother in a nursing home, where he can see in a framed snapshot on the dresser a remarkably girlish young mom, who sang like heaven and tucked him in and looked down upon his face and smiled upon him, and gave him peace.

And then I look at the red Japanese maple leaves radiant with the low morning sun shining through them and think, *This world is so wonderful—it's a gift. I should be writing down three things a day that I am grateful for, I really should.* How is it possible that I don't have time for that?

Sunday, December 5, 2010

Adam comes for his biweekly lesson precisely at 11:00, as always.

Once again I am floored by his learning power. Going over homonyms, I make up sentences and dictate them to him: "They're there, in their house. These two cups of coffee are too sweet to drink, and too hot, too." He spells every word correctly. This is a guy whose native tongue is the Berti tribal language, which has no written form.

After the briefest of explanations, Adam also has no trouble distinguishing "sometimes" (how often?) from "sometime" (when?) from "some time" (how much time?); and "everyday" clothes (what kind of clothes?) from "every day" (how often do you wear them?).

———— ❀ ————

Idly looking over the list of business best sellers in today's *Times*, I come across #9:

Drive, by Daniel H. Pink (Riverhead, $26.95). What motivates people is the quest for autonomy, mastery, and purpose, not external rewards.

There it is. That seems about right. I guess that's what I'm trying to say.

Well, there is nothing you can say that hasn't been said before. This bears repeating: There is nothing you can say that hasn't been said before.

Tuesday, December 7, 2010

I wash my hands in the kids' bathroom, basking in the glow of the new faucet's rich nickel finish. Every time I look at the elegant calligraphy on the white porcelain handle caps, I feel like I've been invited to the black-tie wedding of *Hot* and *Cold.* Here is a mechanism such as the gods on Mount Olympus would have at their sinks—the faucet greater than which none can be imagined—simple, functional, beautiful, true.

As I savor the smooth, wobble-free turn of the tap to its perfect, drip-free shutoff, I realize that this is the one moment of unalloyed satisfaction I can count on every day—a moment that is just as it should be, leaving nothing to be desired. Except—and this does not trouble me nearly as much as it should—when I turn the tap, its sensuous luxury invariably reminds me that billions of people have no decent source of water at all, and for them a rusty pipe delivering clean water would be heaven. Shouldn't I have bought a cheap but functional faucet set and sent off the money saved to dig wells somewhere? Of course I should have, I suppose. I must ask Adam about this.

Wednesday, December 8, 2010

I am grateful for jury duty, time out of time.

I'm in the jury-pool waiting area, at a substantial remove from my daily life. Half the citizens summoned here decamped en masse when invited to pass through a pair of enormous doors to a place where they could present their compelling reasons not to serve. Fifty others have been called to courtrooms. Now a hundred of us remain, sitting in silence, having placed ourselves five seats apart in New York fashion, cooperatively constructing private realms in public space.

To my surprise and delight, the venerable courthouse's waiting area has recently been spiffily renovated. The black Naugahyde seats are in mint condition, the floor is gleaming, the panoramic windows that form two walls of the cavernous room are crystal clear. On one side, milky glass sets off a lounge area with functioning vending machines and clean restrooms with paper-towel dispensers that actually dispense paper towels. Astonishing. I am here, in what people in the future will view as the halcyon days of the past, the time immemorial before this municipal facility attained its enduring state of crumminess.

I am trying to read a book, *Zeno's Conscience* by Italo Svevo, but I am disturbed by the American flag that is flapping immediately outside the window, making an erratic *tap-thump, tap-tap* against the glass. The flag from time to time struggles to horizontal vigor, looking noble and majestic like the flags on TV when stations used to sign off for the night, but it flails in the wind and inevitably falls slack again. Sad.

There is a perfect randomness (or perhaps I should say an infinitely complex chain of causality) to the motions and countermotions, actions and reactions, forces and friction of the roiling, churning, writhing flag—Brazilian butterflies, reality, truth. It's all there, as with riffling poplars or sunlight glinting on the sea: It is what is. *I am that I am.* (Didn't Popeye the Sailor Man say that?)

At 2:50 p.m. the authoritative woman at the front of the room announces that we are discharged from jury duty for the next eight years. I've enjoyed my sojourn on this island in the river of time, but time's up.

Thursday, December 9, 2010

Thinking about the infidelities of the protagonist in *Zeno's Conscience*, I've found a new appreciation for the power of pronouns: The poison of an affair is that it changes "she" to "you" and "you" to "she."

Friday, December 10, 2010

I am grateful for the swim I took in—rarest of pleasures—an otherwise-unoccupied pool this morning. Gliding through smooth, silent water is an entirely different experience from fighting the choppy wakes of others.

"I love it. It's so great when it's like this," I said to Mickey Dunne, the pool attendant.

"Beautiful," he agreed.

"It's like a meditation," I said.

"*Serene*," Mickey said.

There is nothing more pleasing than the perfect word.

In today's *Times* I read that our old friend Richard D. Parsons, erstwhile chairman and CEO of Time Warner, and now chairman of Citigroup, will be a leader of the new "Committee to Save New York," which intends to raise $10 million from undisclosed corporations and anonymous wealthy people to run an ad campaign in support of knocking down public employees' pensions, so that taxes won't inch higher, and NYC can remain a business-friendly place. That is, they want to balance the municipal budget on the backs of working people, to ensure that the city remains a splendid place for rich people—or so it seems to me. I'm sure they see it differently.

Lisa tells me that at the school where she interns as a therapist, a little boy was trying to say something about her to another teacher today, but he didn't know Lisa's name, so he called her "the lady who always has a happy face." *There* is something I am grateful for.

Monday, December 13, 2010
After work, getting off the G train at Bergen Street, *I am grateful for* the departing train's ethereal siren song: three notes, *There's a place* [for us], from *West Side Story*. By chance, the new subway cars' electric motors generate these tones as they rev up, every time. A miracle. For a moment the melody lifts me onto a wave that carries me forward, and everything feels important, and everything feels right.

Tuesday, December 14, 2010
Students have written answers to the questions, "When did you come to the U.S., and why?"

Jovana, a young woman from Peru who works as a home health attendant in Brooklyn, summed it up:

> I came to U.S.A. two years ago because this country give you a lot oportunity for grow up in job and education. I have better life than my country. I can help my family. I can save money for my future.

Martha, who's in her late fifties, recounted the sort of story that Jovana may tell one day:

We came to this country in 1998 together my daughters and sister, because my mother and brothers live in here. My sister helped me find a job in a watch company. Our apartment was very small but my family visited every time and posted a good time. After years past, my daughters have opportunity to study in college, now they are professional and I began to study English in LaGuardia Community College.

Thursday, December 16, 2010

LaGuardia Christmas party: Students, dancing to salsa—first in a circle, then in a snaking line—seem so joyful and warm and supportive of one another. A Time Warner office party it's not.

Ruben, who's already given me a bunch of ballpoint pens advertising the janitorial service he works for, hands me a card signed by everyone in the class. I open it and find $130. "I can't accept this," I gasp, but then I think, I have to, lest I offend them, so I give my heartfelt thanks. My God, hotel maids and kitchen workers giving money to *me*. Well, I'll give it to Make the Road New York, a nonprofit that helps Hispanic immigrants. No, even better, I'll hold onto it and take the class to something that costs money; or I'll buy paper and ink and stop feeling like a martyr when I print up class materials at home.

(My wife asked me, "Does that mean they think you are a wonderful teacher?" I don't know. Maybe they think I'm an okay teacher, and that's just what you do in their culture, like we tip a waiter—it doesn't mean we think he's a wonderful waiter.)

I ask the students to post some party pictures online. I've signed up for Facebook in the hope that we can all keep in touch, so we won't be saying good-bye forever when they leave me. Of course, then I'd have to actually go to Facebook, which I generally avoid.

How much additional misery is there in the world because people can now look at their ex-loves' lives online, staring through a window at the life being lived by a living person, who lives at every moment in another place as though at another time but in fact *simultaneously*—that is the astonishing fact— walking and talking in an infinitely distant parallel universe inches away?

Saturday, December 18, 2010

Muhie, Suad, and I watched *The Wedding*, one of the "We Are New York" TV shows produced by the City University of New York for English-language learners. In this episode, immigrants from the four corners of the Earth overcome language barriers and confusion to put on a successful wedding reception.

"Sometimes, I think that New York is like one big wedding," says Pierre, the Haitian banquet manager, at the end. "Lots of people working day and night to make it all happen: Mrs. Lee . . . Tanya . . . Manny . . . Ramon . . . Carlos, Tito, and Chi. And of course, Ahmed. Without them, there would be no New York City."

Suad dabbed her eyes with a handkerchief. I used the back of my hand. I always get teary watching these little shows, which celebrate New York as a place where earnest, hardworking, warm-hearted people of all nations help one another succeed.

This is a very sentimental view. And yet, practically all of my students do seem to be earnest, hardworking, and warmhearted. Why? Life is hard for them, but life is sweet for them, too; maybe because they can appreciate every little thing they have? They don't know how lucky they are.

Here's a riddle: What do Muhie and Elvis have in common? They were both Shabbas goys—non-Jews who turn on the lights and light the stove for strictly observant Jews on the Sabbath.

This morning as we sat down at the dining room table to begin our lesson, Muhie looked at me seriously and said, "Jimmy, there is something that you said you would do for me that you have not done. You have not found information about Jews from Iraq in New York."

Muhie had told me many times that he had fond memories of his Jewish friends and colleagues, back in the day, before the Jews were driven out of Iraq, and he would like to renew that connection here in New York.

I went home and found the website of an Iraqi Jewish congregation in Queens, and I've promised Muhie to take him out there one day.

Monday, December 20, 2010

I am grateful for the wisdom and good cheer of Jacob, one of the sales clerks at Court Street Office Supplies. When he told me that the pocket-size At-a-Glance Standard Diary I was looking for had been discontinued by the manufacturer, I groaned and lamented, "I've been using that exact model of diary for thirty years. I have my whole life lined up on a shelf in those diaries."

Jacob gave me a rabbinical smile, shrugged his shoulders, handed me the still-available larger diary, and said, "So you'll use this one for the *next* thirty years."

Friday, December 31, 2010

I am grateful for the fact that no calamity has befallen my loved ones. The sword still hangs on its thread.

Sunday, January 2, 2011

I stand on the platform and watch as an F train rolls into the station, car after car jammed with standing people. As the train slowly,

slowly finds its stopping point, like a roulette wheel, the doors open right in front of me and reveal, directly opposite, a little two-seat bench in the corner of the car, with no one sitting on it. "Thank you, God," I say. I always say *Thank you, God* when the universe aligns to provide me a seat on a crowded subway. It's kind of a verbal tick I have, except I say it silently, in my head, the same way I say *Rama Rama* when I kill a bug, or see a dead animal on the side of the road, because a girl once told me that's what Buddhists say to help a spirit on its way. Don't ask me why I do.

Monday, January 10, 2011

Muhie and Suad's son Tholfikar—the one who looks like Elliott Gould and worked for an American company in Iraq—dropped by my house for coffee. We talked about his family's transition from Baghdad to Brooklyn.

"In 2006, day by day the security situation in Baghdad was getting worse and worse," Tholfikar recalled. "While I was on vacation in Egypt, my family said, 'Stay there one more week, because the situation is very dangerous.'" (This reminds me of what happened with my grandfather. He was on vacation in London when his family wrote him that there were pogroms in Russia and he should not come back.) Then their house was shot up, and the family joined Tholfikar in Egypt, where they stayed until the United States granted them asylum in 2009.

"It's difficult to move from Iraq or any country in the Middle East and live in New York City," he told me. "The first six months, it's like, really like hell for me. You feel like not to own this place, you have no friends, you have to build yourself from zero. But it's day by day up to you, you know? You have to figure out how to live. We're gonna try. I think if you really set to do something in this country, you can do it."

Tholfikar—who has a job in marketing for United Healthcare and is studying for the GMATS so he can go for his doctorate in business administration (he has an MBA)—gave me an update on his siblings. Ayass, who moved up to a paid job working the night shift in the veterinary medical lab, is taking tests to get his veterinarian's license. Farah, while working as a receptionist, is studying to be a paralegal. Suhaib teaches computer skills at a school in New Jersey. And Ali, who had a job at an appliance shop in Iraq, is studying ESL at a community college in Brooklyn.

"In Iraq, we have a great, stable situation," Tholfikar recalled. "And one night [he snapped his fingers], everything is gone. Like we have a really big house, and my father, he was working, everybody was working, the best jobs in Iraq I'm talking. And suddenly we lost everything. We are not rich, but we have a stable situation [in Iraq]. And we were happy. And suddenly, you lost all your life. And we start here from the beginning."

"Do you hope to move back to Iraq someday?" I asked

"No, this is it," Tholfikar replied. "I cannot start from zero again. But we'll see. Nothing is stable in your life. You stay like thirty years in same job—" he was talking about me now—"and suddenly you change your career. We'll see."

"Is everything okay for you here?" I asked. "There's a lot of anti-Arab rhetoric, like with the 'Ground Zero mosque'—"

"That's individual," Tholfikar said emphatically. "It's like individual attitude from someone crazy. I never feel like I'm different. This is the power of New York City. We all mix. We are all different; we are all from different countries, so you don't feel like you are different. Like, I'm New Yorker. Like, I'm an American."

"The Americans in your neighborhood aren't angry or upset about all the Arab people coming in?"

"Nah," Tholfikar said, shaking his head. "Americans are nice people, and friendly, too. That's true. I don't know if you noticed that or not. The guy in front of me [across the street] is a very nice guy, he's Jewish guy. And the guy beside me is Chinese. They are always nice with me. And the other [neighbor] girl is Christian; they always send me cards for Muslim events."

Tholfikar related all of this in imperfect but perfectly comprehensible English; he and his siblings studied the language starting in elementary school in Iraq.

I had a question for him. "People ask me, why are you helping Muhie and Suad with English when their children know English?" I said. "I sometimes wonder the same thing."

"Maybe because first of all, I can speak English, but I can't teach someone English," Thofikar responded. "It needs someone he has the skills to do that. I know my mother, when you start teaching her, something change in her life. Once she go outsides, she know how to speak with people: 'How much? How I go there?' I'm talking about sixty-years-old woman. She has zero background in English. She learned a lot. That's very difficult. You have a great skills for teaching. You should have done that from the beginning."

Well, better late than never.

Tuesday, January 11, 2011

The phone rings; it's Reggi, the refugee from Kosovo I taught at the International Rescue Committee.

"I am citizen!" he declares. "I thank you!"

"That's wonderful, Reggi. Congratulations."

"You help me. I remember one time I write it wrong. You tell me, 'Reggi, look at this.' You show me one dollar. I always remember. I tell too many of my friends this. You very practic[al] teacher."

He's talking about the time I showed him a dollar bill as a handy guide to the correct spelling of the United States.

"Maybe my next book I thank you," says Reggi, who's written five. "You help me too much. I never not forget you."

Sweet. I've got to congratulate him in person.

Saturday, January 15, 2011

Reggi was in back changing into his uniform when I arrived at his building, so I had a minute to talk with another doorman, Ubaldo, who used to be Bolivia's vice minister of education. (He was too modest to bring this up; Reggi told me.) Ubaldo confided that he and his family came to the United States only because his wife and then-teenage daughter wanted to so badly. He took courses at LaGuardia in hopes of getting licensed to teach here, but the language barrier proved insuperable. Still, he's got no complaints; his daughter's now an emergency trauma surgeon in Hartford.

Reggi appeared and launched into a vivid account of his citizenship test.

"She ask-ed me six questions, everything is positive. You can believe that?" he began. "One, 'Where is Statue of Liberty?' I say New York City. She say no. I say Is-land Liberty, and she say no.[40]

"So she give me one more," Reggi continued. "Two: 'Who living to White House?' And she tell me to write it: To White House, livin', President. I write it, I forget say liv-*ing*, one 'g'. And she say, 'I take it.' Three: 'Who is first president United States?' George Washington. Four: 'Who is president [governor] of New York?' Patterson. Five: 'From who is Congress?' Representative House and from Senate. Everything positive, but she say, 'Write it.'

"She say, 'Rexhap, I can't read in this.'"

"I say, 'Because it's very hard.' And she say, 'Why?'"

---

40 The U.S. Citizenship and Immigration Services study guide lists "New York (Harbor)" and "Liberty Island" as the correct answers, and adds, "Also acceptable are New Jersey, near New York City, and on the Hudson (River)."

"'Because it's Albanian. Albanian a very old language,' I say, 'and it's very hard teach that.' And she tell me, 'It's hard teach English.' It's talking to her she have opinion I good talk. And she say, 'You are twenty years same job?' I say yes. 'You are twenty years same address?' I say yes. 'Same telephone?' I say yes. I say I have something more. She say, 'What?' I say I am twenty years married, and not wife here. She say, 'Oh my God, you are special man!' For her it's fantastic.

"I tell you, never, never I not forget everything come from you," Reggi promised. "You are very practic. I teach too. I work twenty years teacher. You have some methodology.

"My son ask-ed me, 'Father, you have a problem for talking for citizenship?' I say, 'Yes. Before not going to one teacher, it's very tough. I am going to him, he is very practic. He make it easy, tell me 'Like that, like that.' You give me power, you know. You tell me, 'Reggi you will pass test.' I am one hundred percent I not pass. 'You say no, you will pass this.'"

Reggi ran into a problem after the test was over. The examiner asked where he was from, and Reggi said Yugoslavia, but she couldn't find that defunct state in the computer. So he said, okay, he's from Kosovo, the region of Serbia where he lived, but that semiautonomous territory hadn't made it into the computer either.

"She say, 'No Kosovo, and it's twelve o'clock, I have lunchtime. Please, which nationality?' I say I am Albanian," which was true enough to nearly get him killed, but not so true as to be the country that he was actually from. "She writed there, 'Albania.' And four months he [anyone from the government] not call me, because he take investigation: 'Why you from ex-Yugoslavia come from Albania?'"

Finally, four months after he passed the test, Reggi was sworn in as a citizen, and four weeks later he was in Kosovo visiting his family. "Citizen, you go where you want, no more problem," he explained.

"I have a present for you," I said, handing him a little box, "to celebrate your citizenship." He unwrapped it and found a little souvenir Statue of Liberty inside.

"Exact, *exact*, what I need!" Reggi declared, and I could see from his smile that he meant it.

Saturday, January 15, 2011

PLUMBERS ARE FIXING LEAKS IN OUR BASEMENT. THEY GAVE A $20 ESTIMATE, BUT IT'S BECOME A $3,000 EXCAVATION. ONE OF THEM, GEORGE CLOONEY, FALLS FROM THE SCAFFOLD THROUGH THE CENTER OF THE EARTH, SENDING MESSAGES EVERY SO OFTEN, ALWAYS DATED JANUARY 3, 1979. I'VE GOT ONE MORE YEAR TO GO ON MY SECOND TIME THROUGH COLLEGE. I WENT BACK TO GET BETTER GRADES, BUT MY GRADES AREN'T ANY GOOD.

Wednesday, January 26, 2011

Carlos, the painter from Argentina whom I thought I would never see again, has returned to the class. The construction job in Boston didn't pan out. He's as upbeat as ever, though.

"You can't go like this," he said, bowing his head, slumping his shoulders, and trudging along as though defeated.

Riding the G train home, I realize I am happy. I am good at teaching ESL. It's worth doing. And I'm appreciated. The trifecta. You can be good at something, and appreciated, but it's not worth doing. Or you can be good at something that's worth doing, but you're not appreciated. Or you can be appreciated for doing something worth doing, but you're not especially good at it. But I have all three. And, I have a half-hour ride to and from work on a quiet G train where there's always a seat and I can read. For the first time in my life, I am reading entire articles in the *New Yorker*. They're not always that great; like, tonight, I read a long story about how Fox News chairman Roger Ailes bought a house in Cold Spring, a liberal retreat upstate, and he took over the local paper there, and people got upset. Who cares? Still, just reading the lengthy stories bespeaks the enjoyment of a constructive leisure, engendering a feeling of satisfaction and well-being.

Monday, February 7, 2011

In the hallway waiting to go into the computer lab, I asked Carlos a question.

"Carlos, you once said in class, 'I love my work.' Why?"

"I enjoy." Carlos looked at the wall, puffed out his chest, threw back his shoulders, and smiled, showing how he'd feel if he'd painted it. "Somebody say, 'Look, this plaster no good, this paint no good.' I zip, zip"—he smoothed the wall with his hands—"ahh! Now very good."

Carlos takes pride in his work. Does what he loves, loves what he does.

Friday, February 11, 2011

Ss are handing in autobiographical essays, written in those little blue books schools used to use for tests. Later, I'll invite them to read their stories into a tape recorder for their grandchildren.

Carolina, a waitress in a diner:

My life in Colombia was wonderful, I lived with my family in a big house in Barranquilla. My mother was a sell-woman and my father was a carpenter but now they are retired. I was studying in the college for six year and finished my Industrial Engineering in 2003, while I was studying I worked in a newspaper in circulation department for two years. Then I want to look for new opportunities in other city. I moved to Bogota but the unemployment in Colombia grow up so fast. When I could find a job the pay was really low and I had bad conditions.

Then I decided to come to the U.S. and work very hard. I very exciting for know the snow and see my brother when I arrived to JFK. [Her brother, who was a physical therapist in Colombia, has been a home-delivery man for a Manhattan restaurant for the past six years.] *My brother learn me how take the subway and I did lost sometime but I found the place almost always. I enjoyed the city, the new friends, the shows, the subway, but the winter was terrible for me. I was sick and need come back to Colombia.* [She went home for a few months.]

Here is a new experience, maybe now is difficult because I don't speak english and don't have a good job, but I hope someday the things change for my.

I miss my mom and dad and their hugs.

Yovana, a home health aide:

I came from Peru to the United States in 2008. My husband waited in the airport. He has been here for many years. . . . I started a study training program of home attendant after one month. My husband works in a restaurant in Manhattan. In Manhattan at night is beautiful. . . . I was surprised at the trains in New York. I never saw trains inside the city and under world. My husband and I took the subway downtown and went to and art museum. We saw some beautiful paintings. I like New York.

Pablo, a construction laborer:

I came to the U.S. from Ecuador with my family. I was lucky, the next day after arrive I found a job. . . . I didn't like the food but I like the job's opportunity. I was surprised see many poor people.

Sobita, a Dunkin' Donuts worker:

I came to the united state from Bangladesh in 2008 with my husband. We were working for a company [selling whole-sale housewares and electronics] *in our country and living well. In the meantime my husband got a DV VISA.*[41] *So we decided to come U.S.*

She and her husband moved in with another couple and their two children in a small house in Queens. Sobita got a minimum-wage job at Dunkin' Donuts, and her husband went to work as a night-shift cleaner in a drugstore.

Then I was going to be a mother. I needed a better house. Because tha room was small & one restroom. So I rented a appertment and moved from there.
My first year was enjoable. But sometimes I was scared about the U.S.A. ruls & culture. And I felt too much about my familly. Because my father little sick & my younger brother too. All time I was take cared them. But now is not possible for me.
I thought New York is more clean and less people and more easy to get a job. If I got to knew before my came New

---

41 The Diversity Visa program awards permanent resident visas by lottery to fifty thousand immigrants from countries that have low rates of immigration to the United States. About ten million people enter the lottery each year.

York may be never I came here but now I am little used to in this environment. I miss my family member and some friends. I don't know when I will be able to see them.

Rosa, a tiny, child-sized woman whom her classmates call Rosita, has held three low-paying jobs commonly filled by immigrant women:

I came to the United States from Ecuador in 2005. I arrived alone at Kennedy Airport. I staied with my sister's. The next day I went out for a walk to my nephew and my niece too. It was a weekend. They and I were happy to share together a summer day. At firs weekday, I had to go to work clean office. I worked there for about four months. I quit that work because I felt a little sick. So I needed to change another job as soon as possible. The winter began. There was a lot of snow on the street. I had never seen anything like that. I was so surprised. Anyway I like the snow it's so, so white.

After a few week I got a new job in a laundry in Queens. I was happy because I needed money for the Nativity gifts.

I didn't like the salary, so after a few months I got a manicurist license. I got a job in Manhattan in a nail salon. It was hard for me because everybody espeak English so I didn't understand anything because I didn't speak English, which mean I didn't feel so good then I decided to learn English and bought an English book. And tried to learn English. But now I registered for class. Now I'm very happy because I am studying English very hard everyday so very soon I am going to speak a perfect English and too I am going to find a better job and my communication will be much better.

Sunday, February 20, 2011

Another GED tutoring session for Adam. I asked him why he wants to be a nurse.

"I like taking care of people," he said.

He's had some experience. Last year a big tree-clearing machine fell onto his best friend in Texas—a Kenyan with whom he shared a house—breaking both of his legs and his arm and his pelvis. Adam stayed by his side and cared for him for two weeks in the hospital. (Adam talked with him just last week. He still can't walk, but he's supposed to be able to in a couple of months.)

"You will be a very good nurse," I said. I don't think there's any doubt.

Saturday, February 26, 2011

Drove Muhie to Great Neck, Long Island, to see Maurice Shohet, leader of a congregation of Iraqi Jews that I found online. Horrendous traffic jam on the Long Island Expressway, a frozen river of steel. When we finally pulled up to his house, Maurice came out to greet us, assuring me that our being an hour and a half late had not inconvenienced him in the least. He led us through an immaculate *Architectural Digest* home—gray slate floors covered with breathtaking Oriental rugs—to an area set apart from the rest of the house, for entertaining guests, just like Muhie used to have in Iraq.

Maurice excused himself and returned with little glasses of tea, sesame-and-fig cakes, and bowls of dates. "He'll recognize these from Iraq," he said to me, nodding toward Muhie.

Muhie said to Maurice, in English, that when he was growing up his father told him the majority of Baghdad's population was Jewish. That wasn't far off, Maurice agreed; up to 1950, Baghdad was 40 percent Jewish. But Saddam Hussein launched a campaign to scapegoat Jews. Two of Maurice's college friends were executed on trumped-up charges of spying for the United States and Israel. Maurice, along with every Jew who could, fled the country.

I encouraged Muhie to speak with Maurice in Arabic—so Muhie could be an Iraqi intellectual again, if only for an afternoon. From time to time, Maurice would catch me up on what they were saying.

Muhie told a long, rambling story: While still in Iraq, he had sent a letter alerting the United States to the fact that Saddam was putting jars of radioactive material in residential neighborhoods so that American planes with Geiger counters would bomb those neighborhoods and Saddam could say, "Look how bad the Americans are."

"He thinks the Americans should help him now," Maurice explained, when Muhie stepped out of the room, "but he can't remember the name of the person he sent the letter to. He seems confused. He says things like 'Saddam, may his name be praised.' No one I know says things like that. Even when I tried to remind him of all the terrible things Saddam did, he kept saying it."

This was not what I had in mind when I brought Muhie to renew his old ties with Iraqi Jews. "I hope you're not offended," I said, without much hope.

"Oh, no," Maurice replied with a dismissive shake of the head. "I think it's very hard for him. It's very hard to begin again in a new country."

Still mortified, I told Maurice that Muhie and his family truly were kind, hardworking people, but they'd lost everything after the United States invaded, so maybe it was understandable that Muhie would think things were better under Saddam.

Maurice nodded and said, "I think maybe it's because then he had a job."

Tuesday, March 1, 2011

We're reading *Ruya*, a story about a Turkish immigrant who works in a supermarket. Her boss, who's always criticizing her English, blames her for other people's mistakes and assigns her the most unpleasant tasks and worst schedules.

We did an exercise in which students stand up and go to one side of the room if they agree, and the other side if they disagree, with this statement: "Ruya shouldn't complain about the way her boss treats her, not even to her friends or her husband."

Everybody trooped over to the "disagree" side, except Sobita, the spunky young woman from Bangladesh, who stood alone on the other side of the room. "She should not complain, because she has a job," Sobita said. "A lot of people have no job."

Hats off to Sobita. She believes in what she believes in. Once, when the class was discussing weddings and she said hers was an arranged marriage, her classmates gasped in disbelief, as though she'd been the victim of a savage ritual. Sobita just smiled her delightful little-girl's smile (she's actually thirty-one, but no one can believe it), and patiently explained that the families arrange the match, but if you don't like it, you don't have to do it. She seems splendidly happy with her husband and baby boy, by the way.

Wednesday, March 2, 2011

Sobita came up to me after class. "How do you say this?" she asked, showing me a slip of paper on which she'd printed SWARUP.

"War, swar, swar-UP," I ventured.

"It's sha-ROOP," she said. "It means someone who wants everyone to be peaceful. And it is the shape of our god when our god comes to earth. But after I read Bahadir, I think maybe it is hard to say."

She was referring to an incident in *Ruya*, when a little boy's classmates make fun of his Turkish name, Bahadir.

"My baby came early, so I didn't have time to find a name," Sobita said ruefully. "What would be a good name?"

"*Jim*," suggested her Mexican friend and classmate Irene, half in jest. She was waiting for Sobita; they take the subway together.

"Swarup is a beautiful name," I said. "Leave it for now. By the time he goes to preschool, maybe he'll find his own name." I told her the story I read in the *Times* yesterday about the famous baseball player Duke Snyder. His real name was Edwin Snyder, but when he came home from his first day of school, he strutted around so proudly that his father said he looked like a little duke.

Also, lots of people use two names, I pointed out, one in their own language and one for Americans. "Your little boy could be Swarup and also, say, Steve," I said. "Keep Swarup, but maybe change the 'w' to an 'h' so people can pronounce it correctly. And if they need a little help from Swarup, that's not unusual. My daughter's name is Halley—it rhymes with alley—and everyone always pronounces it Haley, so she just corrects them." (I didn't mention that this drives her crazy.)

"I will do what you suggest," Sobita said.

Thursday, March 3, 2011

After a little online research, I brought Sobita a couple of possible American nicknames for Swarup. "Solomon means peace," I said.

Disappointment flickered across her face.

"And Shawn means something like 'the grace of God.'"

Sobita lit up. "Shawn?" she repeated, emphasizing the *shh* sound.

"Yes," I said. "His name should stay Shh-arup, but his nickname could be Shawn."

"Shawn," she agreed.

Have I just named someone?

Thursday, March 10, 2011

Margarita comes with me to an empty classroom to record her bio essay.

Someone has left the video screen pulled down, so, as Margarita sits directly in front of it at the teacher's desk, I see her face set against pure white framed in black, as though she were a picture of herself and herself at the same time.

I place my little tape recorder on the desk. Margarita smoothes her blue book in front of her, pushes her long black hair off her shoulders, takes a deep breath, and begins to read: "My name is Margarita. I came to the United States with my family from Ecuador. I arrived on October 20, 2007. One month later, I found a job in a shoe store. My job was to attend the customers and help my manager in the inventory each month. In this moment I liked and enjoy my job because I was active in all moment. [She worked eight hours a day, six days a week, at $7.00 an hour.] On February 2008 in my job was a change, my hours downward, the pay was less and I didn't have profit."

Margarita continues her story earnestly, with great concentration.

"I made a home health care course for work with elderly and disability people. I was to study for two months, then in July 2008 I obtained my diploma, I got a different job. My new job is better, because I felt more consideration and respect for me, sometimes I practice English with different doctors. They say me that my English is better each day. I like my job because I enjoy to help at other people, and because in the future I would like to be a nurse.

"In conclusion, I like the USA, because this country has more opportunities than my country."

I hope the children of Margarita's yet-to-be-born children are half as moved by listening to this someday as I am now. I wish they could see the young Margarita, how strong and determined and brave she was.

I mark the tape FOR YOUR GRANDCHILDREN and give it to her. I do this to try to help my students see themselves as pioneers, as founders of American families, as important people whom others, someday, will hold in high regard.

Sunday, March 13, 2011

When I asked Adam if it would be okay to meet on a Saturday next time, he very hesitantly suggested that there might be a bit of a problem: He practices running in Tarrytown on Saturday mornings. A teacher at the New York City alternative public school where he's preparing for his GED found him a coach up there, and he's training to run the 800-meter event.

"Are you training for fun or to compete?" I asked.

"To compete," Adam replied. "In my country I was on the national team. The coach says if I get a GED, he can get me a scholarship to college."

"That's *wonderful!* You are going to get a GED," I assured him, eliciting one of his thousand-watt smiles. "What college?"

Adam took a red card out of his wallet and showed me: MAN-HATTANVILLE VALIANTS, it read.

"That's a very good college," I said. "That's *wonderful!*"

Thanks to Adam and my other students, I see college as wonderful, a decent job as wonderful. I feel enthusiasm. I see life as challenging and full of promise.

Monday, March 14, 2011

Discovery this evening: I have often said that the hallways of LaGuardia Community College's Building C actually telescope away from you as you walk, getting longer and longer as you trudge down them. I thought that this was just a colorful exaggeration, but tonight I noticed that it really does look that way: As you set out down the hall, the last of a succession of arches, at the far end, appears flush against the wall behind it. But as you approach that arch, you begin to see a bit of ceiling between it and the far wall, and then you can see a light fixture on the ceiling, and then more ceiling, and another light fixture, and another. The closer you approach, the further the ceiling stretches away from you, until you can see *eleven* light fixtures. It's a wonder you ever arrive at all.

Tuesday, March 15, 2011

Sobita stayed after class to tell me that she's not happy working 2:00 to 10:00 p.m. every Friday and Saturday for $7.25 an hour at Dunkin' Donuts.

"I don't like this job," she said. "It's too hard. Never for one minute do nothing. If no customer, boss says, 'Clean this. Do that.'

"My husband works overnight at Dwinrid [Duane Reade, the ubiquitous New York drugstore]. It's also very hard. He works overnight so I can do something in the day. It is very hard for us now, because we are only two in this country." One of them has to take care of the baby at all times; they can't afford child care.

Sobita is going to try to transfer some credits from Bangladesh, where she earned a master's degree in world history, to LaGuardia, so she can get started on a degree that might help her get a job here. She asked me what degree she should go for. I suggested an MBA.

Wednesday, March 16, 2011

Carolina came to class carrying a shopping bag with a curtain rod sticking out—emblem of new beginnings. She's moving from her own apartment into a shared apartment with another woman, she explained, to economize. (Carolina landed a $600-a-week job as a secretary to a Hispanic businessman when she first arrived in the United States, but the recession made quick work of that, and she's been waitressing at a diner ever since.)

"In Colombia you had a degree in industrial engineering. Are things better for you here?" I asked her, after class.

"In Colombia," she explained, "the minimum is $250 a month; the maximum is $500 a month. There are many professionals looking for each job. You need, political—" She searched for the word.

"Connections," I suggested.

"...connections, friends, to move up. Here there is opportunity."

Evidently, in the lands my students come from, there is an absolutely fixed class structure. The elite have a lock on everything, and no one else can climb the ladder. In the United States there is the *possibility*, however slight, of improving your lot in life, and for my students, that's reason enough to leave everything behind and come here. They love having the chance to *try*.

"Are you happy that you came?" I asked Carolina.

"I'm not too happy *now*," she said. "The job is hard." She thinks about going back to Colombia, but she'd rather learn English and go to college (again) and then maybe return to Colombia at some time in the future, with money. "I don't know," she shrugged. "Maybe I will be with people here." (She's single now.)

"I'm sure you'll find a way to succeed, because you are capable and smart," I assured her, with all the optimism and confidence it's easy to feel with regard to anyone but yourself.

"I hope," Carolina said, as she left for her shared apartment. "I hope I find a way."

In speech lab tonight we played "All You Need is Love." The students listened and then sang along. I thought it would give them good practice pronouncing the "uh" sound high in their throat (as

in "up") in "nothing," "done," "sung," and—over and over again—
"love." (They tend to pronounce every "uh" from a lower place, like
the "oo" in "good" or the "u" in "rude.")

As I stood at the side of the room listening to my class sing,
"There's nowhere you can be that isn't where you're meant to be," I
was overwhelmed by the feeling that I was in exactly the right place
doing precisely the right thing.

Friday, March 25, 2011

At 5:45 p.m. EDT, I pull over my car (like an Israeli on Memorial
Day) to observe a moment of silence, one hundred years to the
minute after the Triangle Shirtwaist factory fire broke out. It killed
146 workers, most of them young immigrant girls. I end up talking
to the dead, exactly as if they could hear me, even though they are
dead (and would be dead even if they had not died that day), and
even though I am not speaking. *I'm so sorry. You are not forgotten.*
Because of you, we will make sure it doesn't happen again. Thank you
for saving us. I am so sorry we could not save you.

All I could do was teach my class about that 1911 horror—the
locked doors; the vicious, unbridled capitalism; the hard-won labor
rights and safety regulations born of the disaster; the counterattack
on working people that is on the march today.

Wednesday, March 30, 2011

We finished reading a condensed, ESL version of Kafka's novella,
The Metamorphosis. Students trooped to the board to write words
that describe each character ("Gregor—salesman, son, insect,
depressed"). Then I wrote "Character is fate" on the board.[42] As
we discussed what that might mean, I pointed to the example of

---

42 Google tells me I was quoting Heraclitus, but I didn't know that at the time.

Macbeth, but only Carlos, the house painter from Argentina, was familiar with the play. ("Macbeth is destroyed," he said.)

One of six children of a housewife and a mining dynamiter, Carlos dropped out of school to work at construction sites when he was eleven, but he reads every book he can get his hands on, tirelessly attends free cultural events, and drives all over the place to see what he can see. Ask him anything—politics, history, geography, literature—he's got the answer.

Thursday, March 31, 2011

Class party: last night of the three-month session.

Sobita tells me that she and her husband have decided to keep the name Swarup for their little boy. "My husband says it is difficult for us to pronounce American names, so it can be difficult for Americans to pronounce our names. It's fair," she explains. They'll hold the name Shawn in reserve for when Swarup grows up and goes to school.

The students give me a card with $200 in it. It's insane. I explicitly told them not to give me money. (I'll spend it on them.) I'm moved by their generosity and by their words on the accompanying card. Marlene, an elegant woman in her fifties who's a hotel housekeeping supervisor, writes, "I love you." Sobita writes, "You are the best teacher of my life." (This ranking deserves an asterisk, because all of Sobita's previous instructors were in Bangladesh, where the teachers strictly lecture and the students mostly memorize, I'm guessing.)

In the same vein, not long ago I received an e-mail from Sachiko, the bravely striving Toyota-parts heiress, in which she wrote, "You are the best teacher I've never had!! You gave us such a wonderful time!! I will never forget that!!"

Really, I don't know what Sachiko or Sobita could be raving about, other than my being funny sometimes, sharing my interest in words, and always encouraging each student to participate.

I need to become a much better teacher. Students say I am very good at explaining things, and that I keep them interested. But I want to drill and drill and drill on pronunciation, which is their biggest problem and gets insufficient attention from me. I want to plan lessons not just day by day but across weeks and months, purposefully coming around to the same carefully selected vocabulary words, the same grammatical structures, again and again, so students can absorb them through repetition, not use them for an evening and lose them. I've got my work cut out for me.

Monday, April 4, 2011

After we went over the vocabulary in the verse, the class read in unison:

> *April is the cruelest month, breeding*
> *Lilacs out of the dead land, mixing*
> *Memory and desire, stirring*
> *Dull roots with spring rain.*[43]

Tuesday, April 5, 2011

Remember how annoyed I used to be by thirty-year-olds walking down my block blabbering into cell phones? I've come to regard those as the Good Old Days; at least the jabberers pointed their glazed eyes forward. Now people walk down the block with their faces buried in their smartphones. (*The phone is smart, so you don't have to be!*) I make a point of not stepping out of their way as they come straight at me. Why should I have to dodge androids (and I don't mean the phones[44]) as I walk around my neighborhood? I clap

---

43 T.S. Eliot, "The Waste Land."
44 Note to posterity: *Android* was the name of a popular smartphone operating system in 2011.

my hands at the last second or say "*Excuse* me!" to let them know they've been asleep at the wheel, but they don't get it. They just lower their heads and keep staring at their cramped little screens, their tiny six-square-inch worlds.

Thursday, April 14, 2011

Ss, in pairs, asked each other about their jobs and then told the class about their partner. Crysney, a saucy and self-confident Colombian psychology major and diner waitress, worked patiently with Yuan, a bit of an odd man out in the class; he struggles with a stammer that no doubt gets worse when he's trying to speak English rather than his native Chinese. "Yuan is an electrician of computers," Crysney reported. "He doesn't like his job. The salary is no good. He want to be the best 3-D animator in the world." She nodded toward him and added, "He's a very smart guy."

Yuan beamed. He'd just been given that most wonderful present, a good day.

Thursday, April 21, 2011

Each student writes down a secret for the others to ferret out by asking questions.

Rosa has a pet duck. Fabio uses Calvin Klein Euphoria cologne. Martha meditates every day. Flauber has a granddaughter named Brooklyn. Dalia has a sad life.

Sunday, May 8, 2011

Adam agreed to look at something and answer a question for me.

"I love this faucet," I told him, pointing out my pride and joy in the kids' bathroom. "When the old one broke, I searched online and looked at, like, every faucet in the world, and I picked this one.

I love it. Every time I walk by the door, I stop and look at it. See how shiny it is? And the writing that says *Hot* and *Cold*? It's beautiful, isn't it?"

Adam agreed that it was beautiful. I think anyone would.

"But here's my question," I continued. "I spent a lot of money on this, like three hundred dollars.[45] I wonder, maybe I should have spent a hundred dollars on a regular faucet, and then sent the difference to help people—maybe help people in Africa get clean water or something? What do you think?"

"I think it's not right to spend so much on that when some people don't—" Adam put his fingertips to his mouth—"have enough to eat."

"Okay, thank you," I said. "I value your opinion. Maybe what I can do is send an extra contribution to help people."

"That would be good," Adam said.

I knew I could count on him.

Monday, May 9, 2011

At computer lab tonight, Ss searched online to find out who their state senators and representatives were—I certainly couldn't name mine—and wrote to them, asking their support for ESL programs.

The notes ranged from the keenly analytical, by Jaime (who managed a power plant in Ecuador and repairs air conditioners here):

> . . . the learning of English can contribute greatly to the country's economy . . . attacking the phenomenon of unemployment and increase the contribution of taxes. . . . The logical reasoning here is that benefits in the medium and long term are greater than the cost that represents today. In conclusion,

---

45 I couldn't bring myself to say the true figure: $369 (plus tax).

the English Program for Immigrants is an investment, not an expense.

to the politically savvy, by Jimmy (a plumbing-supply stock clerk):

... we can learn better English so could have a better job and so we could pay more taxes, and in the future we could, when we citizens could vote for representatives who supported our program.

to the poetic, by Yuan (a software developer in China, computer technician here):

I am an immigrant. When I set foot on this land, It is deeply attracted by everything here. The people friendly, social stability and environment good. I really love it. I was excited. but I just like a young child. I don't know everything. Everything need to learn. The biggest obstacle is the language. You don't know where to go on the street, phone ring you cannot answer. ... Everything is difficult. The Civic ESL course is just as timely rain to help us.

Tuesday, May 10, 2011
Another Contribution to the Art of TESOL

My friend Gabriel, the begging artist, gave me a pair of Tibetan meditation chimes on a string. You tap one against the other, and *ring!* For a long, long time, they continue ring*innnnng.*

It occurred to me that the chimes' ring sounded a lot like the "ing" that we add to the end of a verb to make the continuous tenses (I am running, I was/have been/will be running)—so much so that the sound of resonating metal might actually have been the source of the verb form.

"What am I doing right now?" I asked the class tonight.

"Talking," "standing," "teaching," various students replied.

"What are you doing?" I asked.

"Sitting," "studying," "learning."

"That's right," I said. "We use the –ing form of the verb because we're talking about a continuing action." (We all moved our hands like bicycle pedals, as we always do to demonstrate the meaning of "continuing.") "I have an idea why –ing means continuing. Listen to this."

I clicked the chimes. *Rinnnnng.*

Smiles of recognition. I think we're on to something.

Thursday, May 26, 2011

Marlene came up to me before class to say that she may be absent for as much as a week. She has to go to Colombia, where her younger brother is in a coma. He was told to have an operation two years ago, but he kept putting it off, because he wanted to finish law school. His graduation is in six months, but now he's vomited blood, and his esophagus and stomach are gone. As she told me this, Marlene started to cry.

"Take your time—it's an expression, it means 'Don't hurry,'" I said, my hand on her shoulder. "Don't worry about class. There will always be a place for you here."

Later, when Ss wrote down what they'd be doing on Memorial Day, Marlene wrote, "I will be in Colombia by emergency." She beckoned me over to her desk, pointed at the word *by*, and looked up at me quizzically.

"*For* an emergency," I said.

"Thank you," Marlene said, and made the change.

memorized the first sentence of the Gettysburg ery American should know it. Only hijab- m Algeria felt confident enough to recite it to , except for stressing one wrong nouncing "a" like apple in "nation." d.

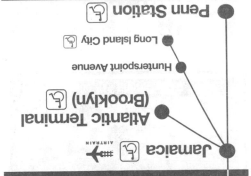

this afternoon at the Seba-Seba works, in Jackson Heights across rocery and Ria Envios de Dinero, , SEND MONEY TO INDIA. There's

lack baseball cap and a yellow nd of her all-day Sunday shift s with her solar smiles and could our food.

nd I came upon the Inner Peace ehind the cash register read

fe we have planned so as to have

—E. M. FORSTER

ow to pronounce the words in are what, if any, difference there nd *were*. It was an excellent ques- ents have difficulty pronouncing y say it like "war" or "ware."

This afternoon an inspiration came to me, just as though it were in the air and I'd breathed it in: My students call me "Teacher," and in that word they pronounce the "er" perfectly. So tonight I wrote on the board,

teacher

-cher

her

were

werek —> work

and I had the students repeat after me as I read down from the top.

They got it! They pronounced every word perfectly. What a breakthrough!

"Now," I said, "we just have to practice. Practice, practice, practice." This called something to mind. "But first, I'm going to tell you the oldest joke in New York: 'How do you get to Carnegie Hall?'" It took a little explaining, but now they all know that one.

I'm very excited and happy—happy, because I'm excited. It's like Yuan told me, when I asked him why he left China, where he had a great job, to come to the United States, where everything is difficult.

"In China, everything is easy," he said, "but not interesting. Come to new place: *exciting!*"

ESL teaching is a new place for me.

Wednesday, June 15, 2011

Ss wrote about what they will be doing ten years from now:

Carolina: I hope I will be married and have a family. I will be an American citizen and I will be live in Manhattan.

Fabio: In my opinion, if God will give my health, I will have a beautiful home in Miami Beach, I want to be retired of my work how mechanic of the Laundry Machines, and to be work how counselor of companies. Also I want to have two children more with my love wife. And enjoy with my family all my dreams.

Rosa: Maybe I am going to travel to Ecuador to visit my family, because I miss them a lot. I also want to get to know my two nieces and tree nephews. I like to take a lot of gifts for them. I hope that they get to be very happy to see me too.

Irene: Ten years from now I hope to visit my mother and father in Mexico because I didn't see for long time. I will be see my son and daughter graduation for the university. I am proud for my childrens.

Thursday, June 16, 2011

I make an announcement to the Ss: Do not give me money when the school year ends next week. Really. Don't.

They look troubled and ask why. First of all, it's against the rules, I say, which is true. But then a better reason comes to mind. "If you want to thank me, please write a card and give it to me. If you give me money, I take it with one hand and spend it with the other. It's gone. If you give me a note, I put it in a book and put it on the shelf and it's there—"

"—forever," several students say.

"That's right. Forever."

Tuesday, June 21, 2011
One More Contribution to the Art of TESOL

I've come up with a trio of statements about rain that I believe elegantly illustrate the three types of conditional statements and the tenses used to form them:

If it <u>rains</u>, the ground <u>gets</u> wet.

If it <u>rains</u>, I <u>will carry</u> an umbrella.

If it <u>rained</u> gold, I <u>would carry</u> a bucket.

Wednesday, June 22, 2011

Ss turn in their evaluations of the course.

There are no complaints.

How have you changed since this class began?

Dominga: Before I was afraid to participe in class. Now not. Now I can answer to the teacher. Before not well.

Crysney: I speak more in English, I understand when american people speak to me. My life has changed evere day. I'm not feel lost anymore in this country.

What can you do now that you couldn't do at the start of the session?

Carlos: I feel more sure. I read newspaper. I can understand maps, book, magazine. I can speak a little and people understand me.

Ouissam: *Talk to doctor make appointments *do shopping alone without anyone *go anywhere ask for anythings *looking for job.

Thursday, June 23, 2011

Center for Immigrant Education and Training farewell party in the cafeteria. The students have brought their best homemade dishes, and a DJ is blasting salsa that awakens me (I'd thought I was awake) and makes me think, "Oh, so *this* is what it feels like to be alive."

I've brought a camera and Jimmy the plumbing-supply clerk snaps a photo as I hand a certificate to each student. I promise to put the pictures up on my Facebook page as soon as I learn how. Then we stand together as a class while Jimmy's wife takes our picture again and again and again with everyone's cell phone or camera.

I open and read the cards the students have painstakingly written: "I am so, so thankfull to you for all what I have learned." "God bless you and your family." "I will always remember you."

I congratulate them for working so hard and learning so much. I thank them for being excellent students who made the class go well. I tell the shy ones that I am especially proud of them, because they used to sit quietly and say nothing in class, and now they speak up.

When it's time to say good-bye, every man shakes my hand, and every woman hugs me. Carlos also hugs me, and I remind him that he's promised to invite me to an Argentine cookout.

"*Pollo*," he says, carefully enunciating the word for chicken. He knows I want to learn Spanish.

I won't have these students in the fall. They've had their nine months.

I desperately want to see them all again. I can't believe I won't see them again. Maybe I will see them again.

The salsa music slowly fades as I walk down that incredibly long hallway that looks like it will never come to an end, but does.

I'll have new students in September.

That expert I heard on the radio saying that baby boomers will end up being greeters at Wal-Mart was half right, in my case. I am a greeter, but not at Wal-Mart. I greet immigrants as they come to America.

I appreciate that there is no distance between who I am and what I am doing, at last.

But enough about me.

ACKNOWLEDGMENTS

I will always be grateful to Sterling Lord, who has been my agent, advocate, mentor, and friend since I was nineteen years old. Sterling was absolutely bound and determined that this book be written and published, and without his guidance and support, it wouldn't have been.

I appreciate the sharp eye and sound judgment of Janice Goldklang, my editor at Globe Pequot Press, who believed this book would be good, and then made it better.

My wife, Lisa, while in graduate school and working a job, found time—often in the middle of the night—to review again and again the hundreds of pages from which this book was extracted. She guided me through the most critical decisions—what goes in and what stays out—and gave me those pearls beyond price: the honest responses of a thoughtful reader. I am eternally grateful and will try to remember to act that way.

My friend Martha Straus, who as the author of four books knows a thing or two about writing, helped pull me through the various sticking points I encountered along the twisting path to this final page.

I owe thanks to the men and women who agreed to speak with me—openly, honestly, and often at great length—about working, not working, and what work can mean. All of them gave me two precious things—their time and their trust. Many of them—such as Steven Stahler, Karla Layden, Wendy Rothstein, Richard Witty, Mary Brosnahan, Gail McDaniel, Mary Rogozinski and Brad Sry—do not appear in the text, not because they didn't merit inclusion, but because I failed to find a way to do justice to their insights and experiences in this slim volume. I am sorry if I have let them down.

Finally, I am deeply indebted to my students, who generously gave me permission to put their words in this book. I thank them for that. I thank them for everything.

ABOUT THE AUTHOR

James S. Kunen is the author of four previously published titles: *The Strawberry Statement, Standard Operating Procedure, How Can You Defend Those People?,* and *Reckless Disregard.* He worked as a public defender in Washington, D.C., and as a writer and editor at *People* magazine before assuming the position of director of corporate communications at Time Warner's headquarters in New York City. Along the way, he has written articles for the *New Yorker,* the *New York Times Magazine, GQ, Time,* and other notable publications. He and his family live in Brooklyn.